PRAISE FOR *WORSHIP FORMATION*

"*Worship Formation* is an invaluable resource for all those seeking greater depth and meaning from Sunday services. Steven Brooks draws on a wealth of experience leading and planning worship to offer churchgoers practical ideas on how to engage the various aspects of corporate worship for the purpose of spiritual formation. This book is a must–read for all believers. I guarantee it will make you want to go to church and help you glean more from your Sunday worship experience."

—RORY NOLAND, Director, Heart of the Artist Ministries; Director of Worship Studies, Hope International University

"Steven Brooks is an experienced worship leader, university/seminary professor, and conference speaker. He knows his subject thoroughly, walks the talk, and practices what he preaches. This book reminds us that worship is a gift of God by which he speaks to us, we speak to him, and are transformed into his likeness."

—WILLIAM LOCK, Professor of Church Music (retired), Biola University

"The Holy Spirit is moving powerfully in our day! Brooks' wise insights and poignant guidance in *Worship Formation* are yet more clear and beautiful evidence of that. Church leadership looking to encourage faith formation more deeply will find Brooks an incisive read 'for such a time as this.'"

—ANDREW BRAINE, President, Worship Resource Media

"In *Worship Formation*, Steven Brooks rightly posits that worship is 'the most important priority of the church' and that through active engagement with worship, and all of the activities involved with worship, we are spiritually formed to be more like Christ. That perspective is at the very center of why we exist and how we are to live—to glorify our Creator by becoming like him. This *theosis*, or becoming like God in Christ, summarizes the entirety of our *raison d'être*. Feasting on Christ the Living Word and partaking of his Body and Blood, we become Christ broken for the life of the entire created order. Nothing is of greater importance than that. Dr. Brooks' love for God and his passion to see God's people adopt a posture of continuing formation through worship is evident and clear."

—JAMES R. HART, President, Robert E. Webber Institute for Worship Studies

"For those who play a role in shepherding our worship gatherings, this book has much to offer. Brooks has clearly articulated the ways in which we are directly shaped as a result of the formative power of Christian worship. This is a clear and concise volume, effectively connecting the dots between Christian liturgical practices and the nature of spiritual formation."

—STEPHEN MARTIN, Assistant Professor of Music, Worship Studies Program Director, Azusa Pacific University

"Worship is both a taste of transcendence and proclaims our witness to the world. The Urdu term for worship is *Ibadat* (John 4:24)—a term denoting both that a worshiper is a slave (*abd*) to his Creator, and that worship is a sacrificial service to glorify God's holiness. Whether the worship be congregational or personal, consisting of songs, Scripture reading, administering of sacraments, sermon, stillness, or supplications, all these help to offer our devotion to the Divine. Steven Brooks' work calls readers to a pilgrimage of experiencing the power and presence of God in worship…. *Worship Formation* is an excellent resource for worshipers around the world."

—ERIC SARWAR, President, Tehillim School of Church Music and Worship, Pakistan

"Worship is more than music, more than sermon, more than Sunday-morning evangelism. Worship spiritually forms us—not just content but experience as well. What are the elements, according to Scripture and the history of the church, that should be part of worship that forms us as disciples of Jesus? In *Worship Formation*, Steven Brooks lays those elements out for us in a thoughtful, passionate, and practical way. He does an excellent job of giving us tools to help us determine how they will form us. Through thorough research, personal insight, and practical application, *Worship Formation* will form you as you prepare worship that will form your people through an encounter with the living God."

—FRED J. HEUMANN, Director/Founder, MusicWorks International; Adjunct Professor of Worship Studies, Ukrainian Evangelical Theological Seminary

"*Worship Formation* is a manual that both educates and equips. So if you're looking for a book that wades past shallow gimmicks and superficial strategies and into the deep waters of faith and lasting change, I invite you to live in these pages for a while, and then live them out."

—ZAC HICKS, Canon for Liturgy and Worship, Cathedral Church of the Advent, Birmingham, AL; author of *The Worship Pastor*

WORSHIP FORMATION

WORSHIP FORMATION

A Call to Embrace Christian Growth in Each Element of the Worship Service

STEVEN D. BROOKS

foreword by Zac Hicks

WIPF & STOCK · Eugene, Oregon

WORSHIP FORMATION
A Call to Embrace Christian Growth in Each Element of the Worship Service

Interior art: Tori Tateishi
Interior graphics: Monica Wood

Wipf & Stock
An Imprint of Wipf and Stock Publishers
199 W. 8th Ave., Suite 3
Eugene, OR 97401

www.wipfandstock.com

PAPERBACK ISBN: 978-1-5326-9634-3
HARDCOVER ISBN: 978-1-5326-9635-0
EBOOK ISBN: 978-1-5326-9636-7

Manufactured in the U.S.A. 02/10/20

Dear Lord, may I see thee more clearly,
love thee more dearly, follow thee more nearly,
day by day.

—Richard, Bishop of Chichester (b.1197–d.1253)

Be sure to check out Worship Quest Ministries.
Worship resources designed to encourage and
enhance worship renewal within the church.
www.worshipquestministries.com

Contents

Foreword

WE ALL WANT CHANGE. Whether it's a car, a device, a relationship, or "the world," for every last one of us there's always something broken that needs to be fixed, something buggy that needs to be optimized, something wrong that needs to be made right. The Bible emphasizes that, despite centuries of human attempts to join or replace his efforts, change comes by the work of God alone. The longer we live, the more this becomes plain. This is because our repeated experiences teach us, mostly through failure, about how change works. We learn that it's not enough just to tweak a few things here or there. It's not enough merely to change our external circumstances. It's not enough to even develop different habits. Failures at lasting change teach us the lesson that we at our very core need something to happen, and that something is ultimately out of our control. Humanity tries hard, though. Really hard. Change always seems like it's just on the horizon.

The Bible uses a rare but strategically placed word that hits the bullseye of true and lasting change: "transformation." Used only four times in the New Testament, the original Greek term is where we get our word "metamorphosis." Two times, the word is used of Jesus—two accounts of the same event, where our Lord is "transfigured" (read: "transformed") in such a way that his real glory is at least a bit more on display (Matt 17:2; Mark 9:2). The other two times, the word is used of us. After eleven chapters of outlining the story of the gospel, Paul says that we are to be "transformed" by the renewing of our minds in that good news (Rom 12:2). And in another place, that same apostle says, undoubtedly referencing the transfiguration, that as we behold the glory of Jesus's face, we are being "transformed" more and more into that glorious image (2 Cor 3:18). I have a hunch that the Bible keeps some tight boundaries around this word "transform" to prevent our self-promoting imaginations from getting away from us about all the possible ways it could happen other than through Jesus.

So here's the punch line. If change ultimately happens through the work of God molding us into the image of Jesus as we behold his glory—if that's how transformation, at its deepest level, really works—then the worship service is the epicenter of world-transformation. Yes, I want to be that grandiose. And I may have once felt the need to prove this to you, but I don't feel that need anymore. Because this book does the job. It buys into the biblical vision of change through worship, and then, thank God, it breaks it down into incredibly useful nuts and bolts. We've needed a book like this for a while now. We've needed a blueprint for change in our churches and in our world that is thorough enough to offer concrete helps and pliable enough to find application in all the different worship contexts where we find ourselves some two thousand years after Jesus's death and resurrection. Soaked in Scripture, and informed by Christians in ages past who wrestled through the meaning of worship with that same Bible, *Worship Formation* is a manual that both educates and equips. So if you're looking for a book that wades past shallow gimmicks and superficial strategies and into the deep waters of faith and lasting change, I invite you to live in these pages for a while, and then live them out.

ZAC HICKS
Canon for Liturgy and Worship,
Cathedral Church of the Advent (Birmingham, AL)
Author of *The Worship Pastor*

Acknowledgements

WHEN I WAS A first-year college student, my music professor Susanne Aultz encouraged me to pray about entering full-time vocational worship ministry after graduation. Her encouragement was a catalyst in my discovery of God's plan for me to be involved in full-time church ministry, which later expanded to the world of academia, to teaching on worship theology and spiritual formation in universities and seminaries, and to the development of my ministry training organization, Worship Quest Ministries.

There have been many people who have poured into my life over the years—teaching, mentoring, and offering valuable advice that has steered me toward the writing of this book. I am deeply indebted to each of them.

First and foremost, to my friend, mentor, editor, and proof-reader William Lock: there is no doubt this book is better for having your eyes look over the pages of the preliminary manuscript. I look forward to our bi-weekly meetings because I know I'm going to be encouraged and challenged in faith and life.

Everyone should have a friend in their life like Andrew Braine. Our countless conversations on worship and the church (even now as we live two thousand miles apart) have made me think deeper and, as a result, have helped shape me into the person I am today.

I am astounded by the scope of knowledge and experience in the area of worship and ministry of those on the Worship Quest Ministries board. More than that though, their hearts and passion for God's church blesses me beyond words. I am honored to serve alongside each of them.

My university and seminary students, both in the States and internationally, continue to offer me hope for the future of the church. They regularly participate in thoughtful discussions and ask deep questions on worship and ministry. I am equally thankful to the churches who have journeyed with me toward a richer understanding of the spiritually formative aspects of worship.

I also want to thank Wipf and Stock Publishers for taking a chance on a first-time author—with my book *Worship Quest*—and then jumping in once again to help progress these thoughts on worship and spiritual formation from my head, to pages of paper, and into the hands of readers. I am grateful for this opportunity.

Most of all: Brooke, Jacob, and Judah. Thank you for your unconditional love, patience with the ever-open laptop and long nights, and the tremendous joy that comes with being part of our family . . . shine for Jesus!

Introduction

And we all, with unveiled face, beholding the glory of the Lord, are being transformed into the same image from one degree of glory to another. For this comes from the Lord who is the Spirit.

—2 CORINTHIANS 3:18

Do not be conformed to this world, but be transformed by the renewal of your mind, that by testing you may discern what is the will of God, what is good and acceptable and perfect.

—ROMANS 12:2

WHEN ASKED ABOUT PLANS for discipleship in his church, a pastor once said, "Just get people in the church and they'll catch on." When I heard this I was reminded of the saying that going to church doesn't make you a Christian any more than being in a garage makes you a car. Certainly, there is an osmosis type of learning that takes place over time without any effort on our part (*sine nobis*, "apart from us"), but simply attending church does not make a person a disciple of Christ. The kind of transforming experience the apostle Paul wrote about to the churches in Corinth and Rome is the result of the right kind of worship. Jesus spoke of this right worship as he sat next to a woman of mixed race beside a well in Samaria. There, Jesus shattered the preconceived what, where, when, and how of worship and revealed that "the hour is coming, and is now here, when the true worshipers will worship the Father in spirit and truth, for the Father is seeking such people to worship him. God is spirit, and those who worship him must worship in spirit and truth" (John 4:23–24).

Jesus tells us the Father is seeking worshipers. But not just any worshipers, those who worship in a right way—in spirit and truth. The first thing we should acknowledge is that as those who worship, we do not initiate worship as if we have a right to do so. Our worship is a response to God's revelation, and furthermore, his seeking out true worshipers. As he reveals himself to us, and we respond to all that he has done, our response is one filled with "astonished reverence, breathless adoration, awesome fascination, and lofty admiration."[1]

Are people today filled with this kind of awe and reverence as they gather to worship Almighty God? Do we indeed offer God awful worship, not in the current meaning of the word that is filled with negative implications, but in the original meaning? In the fourteenth century, awful meant "inspiring awe" and was a short version of "full of awe." So I ask the question, do we offer God worship that is full of awe? A Barna report informs us that an alarming number of Christians claim they do not experience God in a worship service: "Eight out of every ten believers do not feel they enter into the presence of God, or experience a connection with him, during the worship service. Furthermore, half of all believers say they do not feel they have entered into the presence of God or experienced a genuine connection with him during the past year."[2] R. C. Sproul agrees, "People do not normally feel [overwhelmed] in church. There is no sense of awe, no sense of being in the presence of One who makes us tremble. People in awe never complain that church is boring."[3] Our worship gatherings should be filled with awe because we worship an amazing God worthy of "awe–full" worship. Furthermore, as we gather for worship, our great and awe-inspiring God is present in our midst.

> We need to remind ourselves, over and over, that the focus of Sunday worship must be upon the living Christ among us. In truth, if Christ were bodily present and we could see him with more than our soul's eyes, all our worship would become intentional. If Christ stood on our platforms, we would bend our knees without asking. If he stretched out his hands and we saw the wounds, our hearts would break; we would confess our sins and weep over our shortcomings. If we could hear his voice leading the hymns, we too would sing heartily; the words would take on meaning. The Bible reading would be lively; meaning would pierce to the marrow of our souls. If Christ walked our aisles, we would hasten to make amends with that brother or sister to whom we have not spoken.

1. Tozer, *Whatever Happened To Worship?*, 30.
2. Barna, *Revolution*, 31–32.
3. Sproul, *Holiness of God*, 167.

We would volunteer for service, the choir loft would be crowded. If we knew Christ would attend our church Sunday after Sunday, the front pews would fill fastest, believers would arrive early, offering plates would be laden with sacrificial but gladsome gifts, prayers would concentrate our attention. Yet, the startling truth is that Christ is present, through his Holy Spirit, in our churches; it is we who must develop eyes to see him.[4]

Preacher Charles Spurgeon, in his sermon "Magnificat," delivered October 14, 1860, challenged worshipers toward life-changing acts of worship:

Many of God's people live as if their God were dead. Their conduct would be quite consistent if the promises were not yea and amen; if God were a faithless God. If Christ were not a perfect Redeemer; if the word of God might after all turn out to be untrue; if he had not power to keep his people, and if he had not love enough with which to hold them even to the end, then might they give way to mourning and to despair; then might they cover their heads with ashes, and wrap their loins about with sackcloth. But while God is Jehovah, just and true; while his promises stand as fast as the eternal mountains; while the heart of Jesus is true to his spouse; while the arm of God is unpalsied, and his eye undimmed; while his covenant and his oath are unbroken and unchanged; It is not comely, it is not seemly for the upright to go mourning all their days. Ye children of God, refrain yourselves from weeping, and make a joyful noise unto the Rock of your salvation; let us come before his presence with thanksgiving, and show ourselves glad in him with psalms.[5]

Our worship must be offered in awe of who God is which will ultimately result in changing us on the inside and out. And yet, as I write these words, influential Christian leaders have recently announced the renunciation of their faith and have walked away from the church. These examples of apostasy illustrate the importance of worship services that pronounce the truth of the gospel. The apostle Paul informs us that "if anyone is in Christ, he is a new creation. The old has passed away; behold, the new has come" (2 Cor 5:17). It's difficult to retrieve your old corpse after you lose your life by dying and rising again in Christ Jesus. It seems as though these people may have never truly died. The church must do better in offering

4. Mains, *Sing Joyfully!*, 5
5. Spurgeon, "Magnificat," 1860.

worship that leads to the transformation of the inner being because to do otherwise is dangerous for people's souls.

If we are to offer God worship that transforms our inner beings, we must have an accurate view of who God is. Our view of God is important not only to who we are but how we worship. Seeing God for who he is pulls back the veil as we gaze upon the majesty and glory of a God who is beyond our comprehension—for a God who is small enough to understand is not big enough to worship. And so, we stand, or bow with our face to the ground, in awe. And yet, there is something else that occurs when we see God for who he is. In that moment, it is entirely natural that we see ourselves for who we are—sinners before a holy God.

Translators of the English Bible have regularly used only the single word "worship" to translate what is actually multiple words in both the original Hebrew Old Testament and Greek New Testament manuscripts. When the variety of words used in the original Hebrew and Greek is realized, a greater depth of understanding of the word "worship" is gained. For instance, there are some that see the worshiper as an inferior being coming before a superior one. The Hebrew words are *bo* (come), *nagash* (approach), and *qarab* (draw near). Others see the worshiper as one in submission. The Hebrew words are *yare* (fear), *hishtahawa* (bow down), and *sagad* (do homage). And the Greek words are *proskuneo* (bow down) and *sebomai* (honor by a formal act). Yet others describe the worshiper as a servant, serving out of obedience. The Hebrew words are *abad* (service), *saret* (fulfill responsibility to an important personage), and *daras* (seek the will of a superior). And the Greek words are *latreia* (service) and *leitourgia* (public service). In all, these words create a vivid imagery of the way we see ourselves in relation to how we see God. Timothy Ralston states,

> True worship begins with a proper self-evaluation before God, emerges in complete submission to God, and fulfills only the express actions of God. The assumption and conclusion . . . is inescapable: God only accepts acts of worship from those whom he calls his own and who are faithful to his covenant, the Word he has given them.[6]

To worship rightly then we must have a proper view of God when we come before him in worship. Scripture reveals God as he should be seen. As a result, our only proper response is, like followers of old, to respond to God by offering him our sacrifice of worship.

6. Ralston, "Scripture in Worship," 197–98.

Isaiah offers an amazing view of God. Seeing the exalted Lord seated on the throne, Isaiah cried out because of the sin he saw in his own life, and the sin he saw in the entire nation, responding with a declaration of life-service (emphasis mine):

> I saw the Lord sitting upon a throne, high and lifted up; and the train of his robe filled the temple. Above him stood the seraphim. Each had six wings: with two he covered his face, and with two he covered his feet, and with two he flew. And one called to another and said:
>
> "Holy, holy, holy is the Lord of hosts; the whole earth is full of his glory!"
>
> And the foundations of the thresholds shook at the voice of him who called, and the house was filled with smoke. And I said: *"Woe is me!* For I am lost; for I am a man of unclean lips, and I dwell in the midst of a people of unclean lips; for my eyes have seen the King, the Lord of hosts!"
>
> Then one of the seraphim flew to me, having in his hand a burning coal that he had taken with tongs from the altar. And he touched my mouth and said: "Behold, this has touched your lips; your guilt is taken away, and your sin atoned for."
>
> And I heard the voice of the Lord saying, "Whom shall I send, and who will go for us?" Then I said, *"Here I am! Send me."*
> (Isa 6:1–8)

While seeing God for who he truly is, Isaiah responded with a personal confession of sin—which is worship. He also responded by dedicating his life to the service of God—which is worship.

When Moses encountered God at the burning bush, he was told to take off his sandals for the ground on which he stood was holy. Scripture tells us that in response to God's holiness, Moses appropriately hid his face, for God's glory was beyond what Moses could handle (emphasis mine):

> Now Moses was keeping the flock of his father-in-law, Jethro, the priest of Midian, and he led his flock to the west side of the wilderness and came to Horeb, the mountain of God. And the angel of the Lord appeared to him in a flame of fire out of the midst of a bush. He looked, and behold, the bush was burning, yet it was not consumed. And Moses said, "I will turn aside to see this great sight, why the bush is not burned." When the Lord saw that he turned aside to see, God called to him out of the bush, "Moses, Moses!" And he said, "Here I am." Then he said, "Do not come near; take your sandals off your feet, for the place on which you are standing

is holy ground." And he said, "I am the God of your father, the God of Abraham, the God of Isaac, and the God of Jacob." And *Moses hid his face*, for he was afraid to look at God. (Exod 3:1–6)

When Moses finally did get a glimpse of God's glory, we are told that *"Moses bowed to the ground* at once and worshiped" (Exod 34:8). When Moses came down from the mountain and conveyed all the Lord had spoken to him, "Aaron and all the Israelites saw Moses, [and] *his face was radiant"* (Exod 34:30). The revealed manifest glory of the Lord had left Moses changed, both spiritually and physically.

When seeing God for who he truly is, we see that Moses responded by bowing down before the Lord—which is worship.

Moreover, the revelation of John the Apostle not only gives us a glimpse of heavenly worship as the angels, elders, and living creatures declare praises to God, but also provides an example of appropriate response when coming face to face with Almighty God (*emphasis mine*):

> I, John, your brother and partner in the tribulation and the kingdom and the patient endurance that are in Jesus, was on the island called Patmos on account of the word of God and the testimony of Jesus. I was in the Spirit on the Lord's day, and I heard behind me a loud voice like a trumpet saying, "Write what you see in a book and send it to the seven churches, to Ephesus and to Smyrna and to Pergamum and to Thyatira and to Sardis and to Philadelphia and to Laodicea."
>
> Then I turned to see the voice that was speaking to me, and on turning I saw seven golden lampstands, and in the midst of the lampstands one like a son of man, clothed with a long robe and with a golden sash around his chest. The hairs of his head were white, like white wool, like snow. His eyes were like a flame of fire, his feet were like burnished bronze, refined in a furnace, and his voice was like the roar of many waters. In his right hand he held seven stars, from his mouth came a sharp two-edged sword, and his face was like the sun shining in full strength.
>
> When I saw him, *I fell at his feet as though dead.* But he laid his right hand on me, saying, "Fear not, I am the first and the last, and the living one. I died, and behold I am alive forevermore, and I have the keys of Death and Hades. (Rev 1:9–18)

When seeing God for who he truly is, John responded by falling down before the one who is worthy—which is worship.

I wholeheartedly believe worship to be the most important priority of the church. The foundation for this belief comes from when Jesus was challenged regarding the most important command to follow. His reply: worship.

> One of the teachers of the law came and heard them debating. Noticing that Jesus had given them a good answer, he asked him, "Of all the commandments, which is the most important?"

> "The most important one," answered Jesus, "is this: 'Hear, O Israel, the Lord our God, the Lord is one. Love the Lord your God with all your heart and with all your soul and with all your mind and with all your strength.'" (Mark 12:28–30, NIV)

First and foremost, followers of Christ are to worship God with uninhibited fervor. Worship is the church's ultimate priority. All other practices of the church flow out of the ministry of worship and are of secondary importance to worship:

> "The second is this: 'Love your neighbor as yourself.'"
> (Mark 12:31, NIV)

Evangelism, fellowship, service, and all other practices of the church, flow out of worship. As we worship, we are becoming increasingly more like his Son. As we become more like Jesus, we will, as a result, act like Jesus. How did Jesus act? He loved others and proclaimed the good news of that love. Worship is of first priority because it develops us into the likeness of Jesus. Worship is not just one of the many practices of the church, it is the church's definitive practice.[7] All other practices of the church are a natural result of our worship.

Throughout Scripture, we see that the church gathered for worship and scattered for evangelism. We are to worship God first, then tell others about his great love. Over the years I've had the privilege of traveling in ministry, teaching at conferences in several countries. When you fly on an airplane, you are presented with the necessary preflight safety instructions. At the appropriate time in the instructions, the flight attendant informs the passengers about the oxygen masks, saying something like, "In the event of a loss of cabin pressure, an oxygen mask will drop from above. If you are traveling with a child, place your mask on first and then secure your child's mask." The reason for this is because you are no good to the child if

---

7. Chan, *Liturgical Theology*, 93.

you pass out before having the opportunity to help them. I believe this is a good lesson for us as worshipers. We must take care of ourselves first so we can better serve others. As we worship, we are laying the foundation for the other ministries God has called us to accomplish. I'm not saying we wait to tell others about Jesus until we have it all figured out ourselves. The two go hand-in-hand. As we focus on worshiping God, we will be compelled to tell others so they too can worship. God's greatest desire is for all to worship him. As we fulfill our rightful response of worship, all the other emphasis of the church will fall into place.[8]

If worship is God's ultimate priority, then worship needs to be the main priority of the church.

> The Christian church exists to worship first of all. Everything else must come second or third or fourth or fifth. . . . I believe a local church exists to do corporately what each Christian individual should be doing individually—and that is to worship God.[9]

What do we mean when we say the word worship? This is an important question to ask before we go much further. What is worship? There are numerous ideas of what worship is and should be. In many churches today, worship has become synonymous with music. When a member of the congregation comments, "Worship was good this morning," they are oftentimes referring to the musical worship elements in the service. The secular world has even encouraged this misconception by identifying worship as a genre of music. Back when brick and mortar music stores were popular—you know, places you would go to purchase tapes or discs with music on them—you would walk into a store and see the music organized into various genres including Pop, Rock, Country, Classical, and Praise and Worship.

So what do we mean when we say worship? How do we define worship? Searching the Scriptures for a definition of worship will leave us wanting because although the Bible gives us a number of descriptions of worship, it never gives us a formal definition. Therefore, throughout the centuries, there have been many who have attempted to offer a concise definition of worship. Theologians, scholars, Sunday School teachers, and others have all added their thoughts to the idea of worship. Here is my definition that I will use throughout this book:

Worship is our right response to God's revelations.

8. For more on the purpose of the gathering, see my book *Worship Quest*, 49.
9. Tozer, *Whatever Happened To Worship?*, 56, 93.

In other words, worship is when God shows us who he is and what he's done (revelation), and we positively respond in worship (right response).[10] These acts of worship may include music, which is an effective way to respond to God's revelations, but they do not have to be exclusively music-related. There is a statement attributed to Saint Francis of Assisi that states the following, "Preach the gospel at all times and when necessary use words." I would like to say, "Worship at all times, and when necessary use music." Music is a wonderful form of worship, but it is not the only form. We must get out of the habit of using the word "worship" as a synonym for music. Worship does not equal music. Music is one way in which we worship, that is, we respond to God's revelations through music, but music is not the only way in which we worship. To say this another way, music is a wonderful tool, but it is not the only tool. You would never take your car to the mechanic and state that whatever the issue with the car, you only want them to use a single wrench to fix the problem. That may seem absurd, but I wonder how often we have a similar approach to our worship. Just as there are a variety of tools for the auto mechanic to use depending upon the situation with your car, there are a variety of tools for us to utilize in offering appropriate worship to God. Yet, I wonder why we often elect to employ only one way of worship?

Robert Webber states,

> I believe music-centered worship has indeed become a common way of thinking about the presence of God. However, it is an extremely limited understanding of God's presence. . . . The church has always believed not only that God is everywhere but also that he is made intensely present to his church at worship. God is there in the gathering of the assembly, in song, in Scripture reading, in prayer, and especially at bread and wine. Jesus told his disciples that there is a way to remember him (the force of *anamnesis* is to make me [Christ] present). He is right there at broken bread and poured-out wine.[11]

Herbert Bateman echoes Webber's sentiments,

---

10. I say "right response" because there are incorrect ways to respond to God's revelations. For instance, hearing from God but not obeying what he has commanded would be a wrong response; or singing worship songs that express attributes of God that are contrary to Scripture would be a wrong response.

11. Webber, *Ancient-Future Worship*, 133–34.

Authentic worship involves all worthy activities such as praying, reading Scripture, reciting creeds, giving gifts, listening and responding to a sermon, using symbols and drama, and yes, listening and singing to music.[12]

Additionally, we must explain what we mean when we say "spiritual formation." This is especially important since many from various branches of Protestant Christianity may view spiritual formation as a little too Catholic to be quite right. We could eliminate the phrase "spiritual formation," but it would still be a detail and essential element of our lives to be dealt with. You see, as we consider spiritual formation throughout this book, we are not speaking of mysticism, self-help techniques, or spiritual intuition that we impose upon the Bible. We are strictly speaking of the work of the Spirit of God upon and within us. The spiritual aspect of human beings, Christian and non-Christian alike, is continually developing into that which it is becoming, either positively or negatively. Just as everyone obtains an education, everyone receives spiritual formation. The question is whether what they are receiving is good or bad. In other words, is it biblical or unbiblical? This deals with the ongoing work of the Holy Spirit and the various methods God uses to bring about spiritual growth in our lives. For our part, we must take an intentional role in the developmental process by offering open hearts and lives for the Spirit of God to do the work intended.

Correspondingly, spiritual formation is the process in which followers of Jesus Christ are becoming more like him in their words, actions, and responses. This transformation occurs within the deepest part of our inner beings to the point where we naturally respond and interact with situations as if we were a version of Jesus Christ himself in this world. Though it is often initiated by something we do, spiritual formation is ultimately the work of grace, something freely given to us, something that we could only receive as a gift from the Holy Spirit. No matter how correctly our practices are carried out, we cannot predetermine spiritual formation, for ultimately it is the Holy Spirit through grace that forms us and not practices as such. And yet, we are formed not apart from practice, for in worship, no practice or habit is neutral. As James K. A. Smith, professor of philosophy at Calvin College, claims, "All habits and practices are ultimately trying to make us into a certain kind of person."[13]

---

12. Bateman, *Authentic Worship*, 26.
13. Smith, *Desiring the Kingdom*, 84.

Spiritual formation in Christ requires a lot of *re*habituation precisely because we build up so many disordered habits over a lifetime. This is also why spiritual formation of children is one of the
most significant callings of the body of Christ. Every child raised in
the church and in a Christian home has the opportunity to be immersed in kingdom-indexed habit-forming practices from birth.
This is why intentionality about the formation of children is itself
a gift of the Spirit. It's also why carelessness and inattention to the
deformative power of cultural liturgies can have such long-lasting
effects. The "plasticity" of children's habits and imaginations is an
opportunity and a challenge.[14]

Smith continues by offering a tangible expression of this by sharing
the story of Destin Sandlin and his "Backwards Brain Bicycle" invention.[15]
Sandlin created a bicycle with an important difference: the handlebars
work in the opposite way from which you would expect. When you turn
the handlebars left, the front wheel turns right—and vice versa. Sandlin,
having ridden a bicycle his entire life, could not ride this altered bike. His
brain and habits were programmed for a regular bicycle. His "habituations,"
as Smith calls them, had been settled from an early age. Only with extraordinary effort and practice—eight months of practice, in fact—does Sandlin
learn to ride the bike. As Smith says, old habits die hard.

But the story is very different for Sandlin's young son. He learned to
ride the "backwards bicycle" in just two weeks. There is an important spiritual insight here: families and churches should not simply be focused on
informing young minds, but also forming habits early on.

The goal of spiritual formation is a transformed heart, a change at
the inner center of our being, that leads to a life that pleases God. Or, to
simplify it further, it means becoming like Christ. When we gather together
as the body of Christ, we engage in the formative work of the Spirit that
is uniquely distinct from that of personal spiritual formation. The greatest sermons can be listened to by way of a podcast, money can be given
electronically, Christian concerts can be watched online from the comfort
of your home, but there are important theological and emotional benefits
to gathering as the body of Christ in corporate worship. There is something
spiritually formative that occurs when we participate in corporate worship
that is different from the spiritual formation that occurs in our times of
personal worship.

14. Smith, *You Are What You Love*, 64.
15. https://www.youtube.com/watch?v=MFzDaBzBlLo.

I wholeheartedly believe, and propose in this book, that as we respond to God's revelations—through various responses of worship—we are being formed in spiritual ways to act, speak, and be more like the person of Jesus Christ. There are numerous ways in which to worship God, including, but not limited to, music, prayer, Scripture reading, communion, sermon, stillness (meditation and silence), giving (of our lives and of our finances), and baptism. The formation of our inner being as we practice these elements of worship, particularly when offered together as a congregation in corporate worship, is what we will consider throughout this book. My desire is that we will be challenged by the fact that spiritual formation will occur through each element of worship found within a worship service.

FOR FURTHER CONSIDERATION

Theology of Worship

Block, Daniel I. *For the Glory of God: Recovering A Biblical Theology of Worship*. Grand Rapids: Baker Academic, 2014.

Dawn, Marva. *A Royal Waste of Time: The Splendor of Worshiping God and Being Church for the World*. Grand Rapids, 1999.

Peterson, David. *Engaging With God: A Biblical Theology of Worship*. Downers Grove: InterVarsity, 1992.

Ross, Allen P. *Recalling the Hope of Glory: Biblical Worship from the Garden to the New Creation*. Grand Rapids: Kregel, 2006.

Webber, Robert E. *Ancient-Future Worship: Proclaiming and Enacting God's Narrative*. Grand Rapids: Baker, 2008.

Spiritual Formation

Packiam, Glenn. *Discover the Mystery of Faith: How Worship Shapes Believing*. Colorado Springs: Cook, 2013.

Smith, James K. A. *You Are What You Love: The Spiritual Power of Habit*. Grand Rapids: Brazos, 2016.

Webber, Robert E. *The Divine Embrace: Recovering the Passionate Spiritual Life*. Grand Rapids: Baker, 2006.

Whitney, Donald S. *Spiritual Disciplines for the Christian Life*. Colorado Springs: NavPress, 1991.

1

Worship Formation

And the Lord said to Moses, "This very thing that you have spoken I will do, for you have found favor in my sight, and I know you by name." Moses said, "Please show me your glory."

—Exodus 33:17–18

IT HAPPENED AGAIN. I was having lunch with a friend and he said the words I have been hearing a great deal lately. "The worship service feels more like a concert than a worship service." In recent years, this statement has become a common refrain of those attending current worship services. When we get to the place where a concert and a church worship service are indistinguishable, we are of the world and not just in it.[1] Now, before you close this book never to return, let me explain.

I enjoy concerts. I like the energy and the high quality of musicianship which emanates from the platform. I respect the time, effort, and expertise that goes into creating a quality performance for the audience to enjoy. I appreciate the environment of like-minded individuals gathering together taking in a performance of an artist that they like well enough to pay money to see and hear perform. Sometimes, the content of such a concert is both Christian- and worship-based. But we should not be mistaken. Just because the content is about God and may foster thoughts or actions of worship

1. "In the world, but not of it" is a phrase commonly used to characterize the Christian's relationship to living in the world, but not living according to the ways of the world.

does not mean that the event is a worship service. You see, at a concert, the focus is on the performing artist and the production being offered. When you arrive at the concert, the name on the marquee, doors, tickets, and merchandise, is that of the performer. The staging, lighting, video cameras, and jumbo screens all point to the artist as the focus of the event. Even when the event is filled with Christian/worship material, the concert setting is intentionally platform- and artist-based.

In my book *Worship Quest: An Exploration of Worship Leadership*,[2] I detail the differences between a congregational worship gathering and a festival worship gathering. In festival worship, an artist performs worship-based material in order to encourage individuals in the audience in their acknowledgement of God through personal worship (me and God). In a worship service, a worship leader leads the congregation in their collective response to God's revelation by means of corporate worship (us and God).

Festival worship gatherings can be exhilarating. They are designed to encourage attenders to consider God and to offer him worship. But, as mentioned, the festival worship gathering is artist- and platform-based. The artist performs for an audience who has come to see and hear the performance of the artist. On the other hand, the worship service, or the congregational worship gathering, is congregation-based. The members of the congregation are the performers while God is the audience.

In festival worship, value is placed upon the high production quality of the event; while in congregational worship, participation of the congregation is the highest value.

In festival worship, the artist is the primary voice in the gathering; while in congregational worship, the congregation's voice is most important.

In festival worship, specialized audio, lights, and cameras are central to the overall production; while in congregational worship, providing the congregation an opportunity to respond to the ways in which God reveals himself is central.

In festival worship, participation of those in the audience is optional; while in congregational worship, participation of the congregation is expected, and dare I say, required.

In festival worship, interaction with those around us in the audience is an added benefit, but not essential to the overall experience; while in congregational worship, interaction with those around us in the congregation is vital to a healthy time of corporate worship.

2. Brooks, *Worship Quest*, 2015.

In festival worship, the gathering is based upon a specific demographic (age, gender, occupation, etc.); while in congregational worship, the gathering is made up of the family of God, regardless of the demographics.

Much of what I am discussing here comes down to expectations—expectations of those attending as well as those planning the worship gathering. Establishing appropriate expectations in regard to the worship gathering is vitally important. Being in worship ministry most of my life has provided me many incredible memories and experiences, as well as times of conflict and concern. I have received my share of Monday-morning comment cards, phone calls, and requests for appointments expressing concern about a worship service, most of the time, having to do with the musical portions of the service: "The drums are too loud"; "The electric guitar wasn't loud enough"; "The songs are too high"; "The songs are too low"; "my wife's vocals were not loud enough"—(yes, I've heard all of these and more). I have also been on the receiving end of comments from staff in church leadership who desired that the worship service look and feel more like a festival gathering.

I believe these concerns are a matter of expectation more than anything else. Do people come to the worship service expecting to be changed or do they come expecting to be entertained? Do members of the congregation come with the expectation that they are meeting with an Almighty God who has the power to transform lives by the power of the Holy Spirit or do they come with the attitude of "impress me"?

A worship service ought to consist of elements that flow together to guide the worshiper into an encounter with the living God. The worship leader's responsibility is to assist the congregation in its journey toward that encounter with each element of worship within the service serving to reveal God's presence to the congregation, resulting in lives that are forever changed.

❖ ❖ ❖

In our worship, we declare and enact God's story. The grand narrative of God's actions throughout history includes: *Creation*—God created all that is seen and unseen, and it was good. Humanity, however, messed things up and welcomed sin into the world, making it not so good; *Incarnation*—God sent his one and only Son, into flesh (Latin *incarno*), to redeem his fallen creation; and *Re-Creation*—the story is not yet over for there will come a time when God will make all things new. This is the story of God, from Genesis to Revelation, beginning to end, and it is within this story that we live.

A friend, who is also a worship leader, wrote a song which his congregation loves to sing. A part of it has the following line, "As we rehearse redemption's story show us the wonders of your glory."[3] As the people of God gather together for a worship service, the songs, prayers, Scripture readings, communion, and everything else within the service tells forth the vision of God for this world. As we worship, we are rehearsing the story of God. For those that plan and lead worship services, this is the challenge. And it is imperative to rethink the way in which we plan congregational worship. If worship is, as Webber says, remembrance (*anamnesis*—the Greek word for remembrance or a present experience recollection), and anticipation (*prolepsis*—the Greek word for anticipation, or the representation or assumption of a future act or development as if presently existing or accomplished), then our worship services should be planned and executed with that on the forefront of our minds. Do our worship services remember what God has done for us (creation and incarnation) and look ahead to what he will do (re-creation)? When the answer to that question is yes, we will feel the freedom of worshiping God in the fullness of his story.

Our constant emersion into God's story forms and shapes everything about us; "Worship that reveals Christ forms me by making me aware that Jesus is my spirituality and that worship is to form my spiritual life into the pattern of living in the death and resurrection of Jesus."[4] In other words, worship is not what I do, but that which is done in me. Or, in the words of William Temple, the late Archbishop of Canterbury, "To worship is to quicken the conscience by the holiness of God, to feed the mind with the truth of God, to purge the imagination by the beauty of God, to open the heart to the love of God, to devote the will to the purpose of God."[5] In the very act of worship, every part of our inner being is formed spiritually.

As Christ-followers gather in public, corporate worship, there is an expectation that those involved in the gathering will experience some level of spiritual formation as a result of the assembled time together. Many of those gathered for corporate worship may not even realize that spiritual formation is occurring nor that their faith is being formed while they participate in the worship service. Most Christians take in theology through the way they worship. The ancient church captured this in the Latin phrase *lex orandi, lex credendi*, which is loosely translated: "the way in which we

---

3. Walt Harrah, "Here and Now," ©2010 Seedsower Music.

4. Webber, *Ancient-Future Worship*, 93.

5. From Temple, *Hope of a New World*, cited by Hustad, *Jubilate!*, 78.

worship is the way in which we believe." It is common shorthand for the ancient theological principle summarized by Prosper of Aquitaine (Indiculus de gratia Dei), *ut legem credendi lex statuat supplicandi*, meaning that, while worship practices display the church's belief, they also form the belief's themselves. In other words, worship shapes our beliefs. Robert Webber, reflecting upon this phrase, says,

> If *how* we worship shapes *what* we believe, then it is imperative that we pay attention to how we worship. If worship is shaped by culture, it will result in a culturally conditioned faith. If worship is shaped by narcissism, it will result in a *me*-oriented consumer faith.[6]

The songs, Scripture readings, prayers, and other elements within a worship service form the groundwork of the congregation's spirituality and faith. This shows the reality that those planning worship services must pay close attention to the theology in the selected songs, prayers, and other elements utilized within the service. Since the elements of a worship service form us spiritually, worship planners must be sure there is correct theology and biblical truths found in those elements in order to establish a foundation for the right kind of worship to occur. All aspects of worship influence spiritual formation, both for individuals and for gathered worshiping communities. Spiritual formation is anything, Christ-centered or not, that forms our deepest being. Everyone on earth is formed in some way or another, for good or bad, because everything we read, sing, and listen to contributes to the formation of our inner being.

It is important to understand that we are all being formed, at all times. It is not a question as to whether or not we are being formed, it is a question of how we are being formed. Healthy spiritual formation occurs when we allow the Holy Spirit to mold our hearts and lives. Poor spiritual formation occurs when we try to manipulate formation or participate in weak, inaccurate theological efforts. When we hear of Christians falling away from the faith and leaving the church, it suggests that they have been poorly catechized and poorly formed by the worship within their churches. This is not just a problem within evangelicalism, but something all Christians must face and all leaders of worship must consider. Our sacred liturgies[7]

---

6. Webber, *Ancient-Future Worship*, 104.

7. Liturgy, from the Greek word *leitourgia*, simply means the work or action of worship/service, or some would say "the work of the people" (the literal translation of the two words "litos ergos" or "public service," that which we do in a worship service). For

must be theologically strong and infused with scriptural truth in order for us to grow in faith and relationship with Jesus Christ.

Yet sacred liturgies are not the only liturgies available to people. There are also secular liturgies that vie for our attention. One simply needs to attend a national football league game in Green Bay, Wisconsin to understand the power of cultural formation. Grown men and women attend this sporting event with their favorite players' jerseys on, painted faces, screaming with all their might in support of their favorite team. Some even wear foam hats in the shape of cheese. These zealous fans have been formed by the secular liturgy of sport. To further illustrate this point, an organization called *Religion of Sports* states on their website, "Sports aren't like religion. Sports are religion. They provide meaning, purpose, and significance to their participants—from athletes to spectators, coaches to broadcasters, to family, friends, and fans. If sports are the faith, these are the faithful—and we are its disciples." From cofounders Tom Brady, Michael Strahan, and Gotham Chopra, *Religion of Sports* "seeks to explore how sports can deeply influence societies around the world, why they matter, and how they give fans an experience bordering on the religious." The same can be said for secular music and/or art as fans swoon and some even faint while their favorite musician is performing a concert—just search for videos of Beatles, Michael Jackson, or Justin Bieber concerts.

Advertisers fully understand this concept of cultural formation and utilize it remarkably well. They intentionally spend millions of dollars on advertisements in order to get us to believe that this product or that idea will change our lives for the better.

It is commonly understood that there are two main realms of a person's life—home (known as the first place) and work (the second place). It has been suggested, however, that for a healthy existence, people must live in a balance of three realms: home life, the workplace, and the inclusively sociable places.[8] The idea of a third place to socialize, outside of home and work, led to the development of the term "Third Places." These third places are where people can gather, outside of home and work, to put aside

---

some, especially in Protestant evangelical traditions, "liturgy" may sound like a bad word. It's filled with connotations that make us suspicious. It may insinuate vain repetition and empty religious practice. What's interesting is that the Protestant Reformers had those same reservations about medieval Catholic worship. But their response, rather than being anti-liturgical, was to participate in proper liturgy. The problem wasn't liturgy per se, but dysfunctional liturgies.

8. See Oldenburg, *Great Good Place*, and Putnam, *Bowling Alone*.

the concerns of those two places, and engage with others simply for the pleasure of good company and lively conversations. Third places are at the heart of a community's social vitality.

Third places are environments such as churches, coffee shops, clubs, public libraries, or parks. In his book *The Great Good Place*, Ray Oldenburg argues that third places are important for civil society, democracy, civic engagement, and establishing feelings of a sense of place. They offer strong personal and communal benefits to those who participate in third place socializing. These places are a global element, not specific to a culture or region. In addition, we see that third places have historical precedent and impact:

• The Agora (gathering or market place) in Greece

• The American tavern during the American Revolution

• The French café during the French Revolution

• The London pubs during the Enlightenment

• Starbucks in modern-day United States

There are some within the computer and internet industry that have declared that third places are shifting to the virtual world as well—virtual third places.[9] This practice is easily adopted because of the similarities in characteristics found between the virtual and physical worlds. With the increasing popularity of online multiplayer video games, individuals from across the globe are becoming more connected with each other. The potential for social culture clashes is inherently high considering the large volume of interactions of users from different cultures. However, the online virtual communities constructed within these games share the same characteristics with traditional third places. One of the more prominent features of these communities is the social equalizing aspect. These games allow users to interact through their in-game character, or avatar, which serves as a medium for the player and removes the player's social identifiers. Avatars often interact via built-in chat systems, allowing users to communicate without revealing their identity through their voice. Therefore, any type of social identification is dependent upon the avatar, not the actual player. As users play more, they are accepted into the community by fellow gamers, forming new social bonds.

There is no doubt that we are formed by various liturgies in our lives, whether sacred or secular, physical or virtual. The important thing is to realize

9. Soukup, "Computer-Mediated Communication."

that it is occurring and to be aware of what we are allowing to form within us. As followers of Christ, it is imperative that we respond to God through acts of right worship, allowing the Spirit of God to form our hearts and to transform our minds. "It is true that while we worship God, we are also being formed into God's people. While we are attempting to see God, we are acquiring, as a kind of by-product, a vision of who we are and who we are meant to be."[10]

We do not worship God with the intention of receiving good will from God, but it is undeniable that when we worship God in a right and proper way, good things happen in our lives. This is seen throughout the history of God's people. Take the nation of Israel under the prophet Haggai's leadership as one such example. God speaks through Haggai to show the people that because they have been defiled by their sin, they could not receive the fullness of God's blessings. Yet when they turned from their sins, God told them that he would bless them "from this day on" (Hag 2:10–19).

God blesses those who worship rightly. The greatest blessing received for those who worship rightly is the gift of knowing God. This is further enhanced through our worship as we experience the presence of God in our midst. Moses experienced this firsthand as he encountered God and received the promise of God's presence. Moses cried out with a desire to know God and for God to be known in him. The Lord agreed giving Moses the promise of his presence. This was a communal promise, not just for Moses, but also for the entire nation of Israel:

> Moses said to the Lord, "See, you say to me, 'Bring up this people,' but you have not let me know whom you will send with me. Yet you have said, 'I know you by name, and you have also found favor in my sight.' Now therefore, if I have found favor in your sight, please show me now your ways, that I may know you in order to find favor in your sight. Consider too that this nation is your people." And he said, "My presence will go with you, and I will give you rest." And he said to him, "If your presence will not go with me, do not bring us up from here. For how shall it be known that I have found favor in your sight, I and your people? Is it not in your going with us, so that we are distinct, I and your people, from every other people on the face of the earth?"
>
> And the Lord said to Moses, "This very thing that you have spoken I will do, for you have found favor in my sight, and I know you by name." Moses said, "Please show me your glory." (Exod 33:12–18)

10. Willimon, *Service of God*, 43.

As we gather as a community of faith in the presence of God, we gather with the expectation to worship God, responding to his revelation. Correspondingly, as we worship God throughout a worship service, amidst all elements of worship, we are being formed spiritually. Yet many of today's Protestant evangelical churches have disregarded the potential of spiritual formation to occur within each element of the worship service. Instead, the sermon has been given the most esteemed place of honor. Worship services have been planned with each element of worship (songs, prayers, giving, communion, Scripture reading, etc.) coordinated to point to the sermon as that which holds the entire service together. All other worship elements have been relegated to pave the way for the preaching thus encouraging the mentality that they are preliminaries, or postscripts, to the main event—the sermon.

Our lives, however, should be spiritually formed by our participation in each of the elements of the worship service, not just the sermon. The sermon should be seen as one offering among many during the corporate gathering. Preaching is not the center of the service which all other elements of worship point to. Nor is it the high point of the service that towers over the readings, communion, or the singing of songs, because in fact, spiritual formation is at stake in all of these actions. "From the beginning of the service to the end, our eyes are open to God's glory and our ears to God's truth."[11] There are no preliminaries to get out of the way. Each element in the worship service is an act of worship offered to God, and as such serves to form us spiritually. As we worship through music, prayer, Scripture reading, communion, sermon, stillness, giving, and baptism, we are engaged in spiritual formation.

SPIRITUAL FORMATION

baptism *prayer* *communion* *giving* *music* *stillness* *scripture reading* *sermon*

11. Wiersbe, *Real Worship*, 127.

Given the significance of worship, we must consider every aspect of a worship service to be essential. In his letter to the church in Corinth, the apostle Paul describes such a worship service:

> But if all prophesy, and an unbeliever or outsider enters, he is convicted . . . and so, falling on his face, he will worship God and declare that God is really among you. (1 Cor 14:24–25)

Here, Paul is describing a worship service that has a transforming effect on the lives of people. Lives are transformed by the power of the Holy Spirit and those present are convicted of their sins and called to accountability. As a result of experiencing this transforming power, they fall on their face and worship God.

Dallas Willard says, "Spiritual formation for the Christian refers to the Spirit-driven process of forming the inner world of the human self so that it becomes like the inner being of Christ himself."[12] Henri Nouwen claimed spiritual formation as knowing the heart of Jesus and loving him, which Nouwen claimed is the same thing.[13] I use the term *worship formation*—we are becoming more like Christ (spiritual formation) as we respond to his revelations (worship).

If we are to understand how spiritual formation occurs within each element of the worship service, we must look at each element in light of spiritual formation. How does music form us spiritually? How about prayer; Scripture reading; communion; sermon; stillness; giving; baptism? Is it possible for these elements of worship to be a catalyst in the making of disciples? Is this a worthwhile exploration, or is the sermon enough? These and more are the questions we will explore on this journey toward *worship formation* as we look at how each element of a worship service has the potential to spiritually form the life of the worshiper.

CONSIDER THIS

After a worship service, meet with those responsible for planning worship. Ask one another about God encounters in the worship service. Share the worship element in which you experienced the presence of God most strongly (a prayer, the lyrics of a song, a Scripture reading, a part of the sermon, communion, etc.). Prayerfully decide on ways to enhance opportunities for the formation of the congregation through the various elements of your worship service.

12. Willard, *Renovation of the Heart in Daily Practice*, 15.

13. Nouwen, *In the Name of Jesus*, 41.

2

Music as an Act of Worship

Let the word of Christ dwell in you richly, teaching and admonishing one another in all wisdom, singing psalms and hymns and spiritual songs, with thankfulness in your hearts to God.

—COLOSSIANS 3:16

IT WAS THE SUMMER of 1991. I was a teenager who knew everything . . . or so I thought. Surprising, right? The church secretary called my house and told me that because of a scholarship, the cost for me to go to summer camp was covered, if I wanted to go. I asked if my best friend would also be able to go. She said she was sorry, but they only had enough for one scholarship. I told her thanks, but no thanks. I wasn't going to camp without my best friend.

A short while later the phone rang once more. It was the church secretary calling again. She said someone gave more to the scholarship account and it was enough for both my best friend and I to go to camp. Later, I would find out that after hanging up with me the first time, she called my friend and he told her that he wouldn't accept the scholarship because he didn't want to go to camp without me. I never did find out who gave the extra money for both of us to go, but I wouldn't be too surprised if she gave it herself.

So we both arrived at camp—my best friend and I. I wish I could tell you we were the perfect campers, grateful that someone paid for us to go to camp, but I can't. In fact, we did everything in our power to not enjoy the camp experience—complete with bad attitudes. It was definitely not my best time. We wouldn't participate in the cabin discussions and we refused to be involved in the recreation time. We pretty much didn't participate in anything and I acted as though I didn't want to be there, making sure everyone knew. In my opinion, the only good thing about camp, were the cute girls. I was sure I wouldn't get anything out of the week, but I figured I could bear with it. God, on the other hand, had another plan.

One midweek evening, I sat in the mountain chapel of that Christian summer camp listening to the band lead worship. I don't remember the speaker, or his talk, but the band is still a vivid memory. At the end of that chapel time, the bandleader gave an altar call for those who wanted to give their lives to Christ, and for those who needed to rededicate their lives to the Lord. That night, it became evident that although I knew a good amount about God, my relationship with him needed some improvement. I possessed a lot of head knowledge, but I was disconnected from God in my heart and from what God wanted for my life. I immediately sat down with my cabin counselor and renewed my commitment to have God be the Lord of my life. It was an evening that has forever changed my life; a moment that God had orchestrated.

That evening in chapel, it was the music, not the sermon, which God used to challenge me. From that experience, I became aware of how the Spirit of God uses music as a tool for spiritual formation in one's life, and I made a commitment to the Lord that I would follow his leading.

❖ ❖ ❖

The church's song is about story. Throughout Scripture we find that when God's people remembered his saving acts, they invariably sang. After their deliverance from Egypt, Miriam, Moses, and the people sang (Exod 25:1–8). When David prepared a place for the Ark of the Covenant, he appointed musicians who sang a song of thanksgiving (1 Chr 16:8–34). Angels sang of the glory of God at the birth of Jesus (Luke 2:14). And at the conclusion of the story, throughout the book of Revelation, there is song. The reason for the song is to tell the story of God's mighty acts. Music is a primary means by which the body of Christ remembers, celebrates, and declares what God has done.

The songs in our worship services are to a large degree formative. A congregation learns its theology not just by the preaching they hear, but also by the songs they sing. "We are far more likely to find ourselves humming something we sang in church when we go home than we are to find ourselves meditating on a phrase in the sermon," observes Rosalind Brown.

"Words set to music engage the emotions and lodge in the memory. The refrains of hymns and choruses are even more likely to stick in the mind, simply because they are sung more frequently."[1] In the previous chapter we looked at the phrase

> *lex orandi, lex credendi*
> the way in which we worship is the way in which we believe.

An adaptation of that phrase is

> *lex cantandi, lex credendi*
> the way in which we sing is the way in which we believe.

The songs we sing in church embed themselves into our minds as truth and engrave themselves upon our hearts. There have been times when I have had conversations with people concerning issues of faith and they begin, without realizing, to quote song lyrics as a defense for what they believe. The words of the songs they have sung over the years in worship have become an important part of their belief system. In some cases, song lyrics have re-placed Scripture as a defense for what we believe and why we believe it.

The human mind is complex and formed in ways that are still not entirely understood. Research has shown the power of music's effect upon the mind not just as we grow and learn, but even as one grows older or is stricken with mental disabilities. Music has been found to stimulate parts of the brain, and studies have shown that music even enhances the memory of Alzheimer's and dementia patients, including a study conducted at University of California Irvine, which revealed that scores on memory tests of Alzheimer's patients improved when they listened to classical music.[2] In addition, research has shown that there are cognitive and neural benefits of musical experience that continue throughout one's life, and, in fact, has the potential to counteract some of the negative effects of aging, such as memory and hearing difficulties in older adults.[3] It is easy to undervalue the extent of enduring faith among elderly people, who may have through-out their lifetime subconsciously learned by heart a core repertoire of hymns (and songs). When patients with dementia sing these songs again,

---

1. Brown, *How Hymns Shape Our Lives*, 21.
2. Lucas, "Boost Memory and Learning with Music."
3. Parbery-Clark et al., "Musical Experience and Hearing Loss."

confusion seems to disappear, and it appears as though they are able to reenter the world of lucidity and understanding once more.[4]

Moreover, the singing of worship songs at the bed of a dying Christian has a powerful impact upon the anticipated moment of crossing the threshold of leaving this world and meeting Jesus. Even those who have been too weak to speak or interact have been known to respond positively to the singing of worship songs. This practice of singing at the deathbed is not a new practice. French Benedictine monks, for example, were using Gregorian chants in the Middle Ages to bring comfort to the dying. Singing songs of worship at the bed of a dying Christ-follower is based on the understanding that music can bring comfort to both the dying and the loved ones left behind.

Music and songs have an impact not only on our physical and mental capacities, but the songs of worship we sing also form our beliefs beyond our realization. We gain understanding of God and assurance of our faith. John Wesley wrote, "I would recommend [the hymnbook] to every truly pious reader: as a means of raising or quickening the spirit of devotion, of confirming the faith, of enlivening his hope, and of kindling or increasing his love to God and man."[5] Martin Luther considered his people "theological barbarians" and so taught them basic theology by devoting Thursday evenings to congregational hymn singing.[6] The editors of the old Trinity Hymnal state in the preface, "It is well known that the character of its song, almost equal with the character of its preaching, controls the theology of the church."[7] The songs we sing in our worship services must be theologically and biblically sound, otherwise we may be teaching our congregation false theology or heretical doctrine.

The saying "Let me write the songs of a nation, and I care not who writes its laws" is often attributed to Plato[8] who understood the power of songs to shape the beliefs and lives of people. This understanding is particularly true of the church: Let me write the songs of the church, and I care little who writes its theology.[9] The opponents of the Reformation were accurate

---

4. Deans, "Hymns and Ministry to Those with Dementia."

5. Wesley in the preface to the 1780 handbook, para. 8. Quoted in Brown, *How Hymns Shape Our Lives*, 6.

6. Bainton, *Life of Martin Luther*, 267.

7. Orthodox Presbyterian Church, *Trinity Hymnal*, vi.

8. Although some attribute this quote to Plato, others accredit the saying to Scottish writer, politician, and patriot Andrew Fletcher (b. 1653–d. 1716).

9. Dale, *Nine Lectures on Preaching*, quoted in Segler and Bradley, *Christian Worship*, 106.

when they complained, "Luther has done us more harm by his songs than by his sermons." It's true that we often learn our theology first from the songs we sing, long before we even remember a sermon. The story at the beginning of this chapter of how music formed me spiritually is not unique to me. Countless others have expressed how music has been used to enlighten their minds toward a greater understanding of God. As a pastoral leader, there have been numerous times when a member of the congregation shared that it was within the music of the worship service that God revealed himself to them and spiritual formation occurred within his or her life.

Father Joseph Gelineau, a French church musician whose songs were widely used, believed music gives meaning to worship by its service to the worshiping congregation, inviting them to greater faith, hope, and love of the mystery of Jesus Christ.[10] Erik Routley, a minister and musician from Britain, suggests that the music of worship should point to the death and resurrection of Christ, lead worshipers to a greater maturity in Christ, and spur the congregation to the building of God's kingdom.[11] The Eastern Orthodox Church often takes the view that music can "reflect the harmony of heaven" and "can provide us with a foretaste of the splendor of the Age to come."[12]

I began this discussion by stating that songs in our worship services are to a great degree formative. One such song that forms the worshiper as they sing is "One Day."[13] As the singer expresses the words of the hymn, they journey through God's story, learning basic theology and gaining a greater understanding of God's love for humanity.

> One day when heaven was filled with his praises
> One day when sin was as black as could be
> Jesus came forth to be born of a virgin
> Dwelt amongst men, my example is he!
>
> One day they led him up Calvary's mountain
> One day they nailed him to die on the tree
> Suffering anguish, despised and rejected
> Bearing our sins, my Redeemer is he!

10. Pottie, *More Profound Alleluia!*, 26–27.
11. Pottie, *More Profound Alleluia!*, 61.
12. Archbishop John, "Sacred Music," 3.
13. "One Day," by J. Wilbur Chapman, 1910, public domain.

One day they left him alone in the garden
One day he rested, from suffering free
Angels came down o'er his tomb to keep vigil
Hope of the hopeless, my Savior is he!

One day the grave could conceal him no longer
One day the stone rolled away from the door
Then he arose, over death he had conquered
Now is ascended, my Lord evermore!

One day the trumpet will sound for his coming
One day the skies with his glories will shine
Wonderful day, my beloved ones bringing
Glorious Savior, this Jesus is mine!

Living, he loved me; dying, he saved me
Buried, he carried my sins far away
Rising, he justified freely, forever
One day he's coming—O, glorious day!

"Come Behold the Wondrous Mystery,"[14] a theologically rich song leading the worshiper through the story of God's redemptive work, is an example of a modern song that helps spiritually form the worshiper as they sing. Observe the richness of scriptural language and symbolism throughout the song's lyrics.

Come behold the wondrous mystery in the dawning of the King
He the theme of heaven's praises robed in frail humanity
In our longing, in our darkness now the Light of Life has come
Look to Christ, Who condescended took on flesh to ransom us

Come behold the wondrous mystery he the perfect Son of Man
In his living, in his suffering never trace nor stain of sin
See the true and better Adam come to save the hell-bound man
Christ the great and sure fulfillment of the law; in him we stand

14. "Come Behold the Wondrous Mystery," words and music by Matt Boswell, Matt Papa, Michael Bleecker © 2013 Getty Music Songs, LLC ASCAP designee, McKinney Music Inc. (BMI) (Adm by MusicServices.org) / Love Your Enemies Publishing (ASCAP) / Bleecker Publishing (ASCAP)

Come behold the wondrous mystery Christ the Lord upon the tree
In the stead of ruined sinners hangs the Lamb in victory
See the price of our redemption see the Father's plan unfold
Bringing many sons to glory grace unmeasured, love untold

Come behold the wondrous mystery slain by death the God of life
But no grave could e'er restrain him praise the Lord; He is alive!
What a foretaste of deliverance how unwavering our hope
Christ in power resurrected as we will be when he comes

As the worshiper sings truths found within such songs, their theology is founded and their faith is strengthened, resulting in positive formation of their inner being. It is unfortunate, however, that many of the songs sung in our churches today do not focus on God and his story, but rather focus on self. A quick study of many of the recent songs of worship reveals a view of worship that is not centered on God's story, but on the worshiper. There may not particularly be any heresy within the song, but it comes more from a narcissistic view of God rather than Scripture. Many of these songs are offered to God, but God often remains nameless in the song lyrics. Throughout such songs the singer is never informed of whom they are singing to. This is not to say that these songs which do not name God should never be sung in worship.[15] But if this is the only manner of song employed, how will the worshiper be spiritually formed in a truly significant way? Furthermore, by not naming God, specifically the three persons of the Trinity—Father, Son, and Holy Spirit—some wonder if the song can truly be called a "Christian" song.

The Trinity is a chief Christian doctrine duplicated by no other religion in the world. It is a primary way Christian worship is defined to be Christian. If our worship then, is to be Christian worship, it must be trinitarian, acknowledging all three persons of the Godhead. I recognize that not every song needs to instruct in extensive ways, but that should not mean that any song should be exempt from operating out of a trinitarian perspective. Yet, many of the songs sung in worship do not mention the Trinity and many choose to employ general terms such as you, God, and

---

15. Such songs could be incorporated into the worship service when 1) they are preceded by the reading of Scripture or a prayer as to remove any doubt to whom the song is to be sung; 2) they are surrounded by songs and/or other elements of worship that are theologically rich.

Lord[16], rather than incorporate several of the nearly one thousand names of God found throughout the pages of Scripture.

This topic is of particular interest to worship historian Dr. Lester Ruth. Some years ago he published an article examining and lamenting the general absence of the Trinity in CCLI's top twenty-five song lists from 1989–2004.[17] In his research he found that there were only three songs that made explicit reference to all three persons of the Trinity, only a few that explicitly referenced the Father and the Spirit, and the largest number referencing Jesus or "God" abstractly. One of the conclusions he drew from his observations is that evangelical theology couldn't be said to be trinitarian if you evaluated this from its music alone . . . and it certainly isn't forming its people in an orthodox trinitarian way through its worship music. Dr. Ruth says,

> In a variety of ways these songs (CCLI lists) rarely contribute to the development of a trinitarian faith. Take the issue of naming the Father, the Son, and the Holy Spirit, for example. None of the songs refer to the Trinity or the triune nature of God. And only three songs refer to all three Persons of the Trinity: "Glorify Thy Name," "Father I Adore You," and "Shine Jesus Shine." This lack of naming is most obvious in the absence of references to God the Father and the Holy Spirit. Only four songs speak of God as Father and only six refer to the Spirit.[18]

Before we jump to the conclusion that this is a new issue with contemporary worship choruses, we must acknowledge that many older hymns and gospel songs are similar in mentioning, or rather, not mentioning the Trinity. In further analysis, Ruth compared the worship songs that topped the CCLI lists with the most printed evangelical hymns and gospel songs between 1737 to 1860, as surveyed by Stephen Marini in his work "Hymnody as History". Ruth found that only three hymns (the same amount as the contemporary praise songs on the lists) explicitly reference all three persons of the Trinity while most focus on the second person, Jesus. As a result, it can be said that both traditional and contemporary songs are equally weak in referencing the Trinity—and equally strong in addressing Jesus.

16. If a song employs only the terms you, God, or Lord in the lyrics, how do we know the song is a Christian song and not a song of a different religion, since many of them address their deity as god and lord as well?

17. CCLI is Christian Copyright Licensing International

18. Ruth, "Don't Lose the Trinity," para. 3.

Dr. Ruth challenged worship song writers to craft songs that mention all three persons of the Trinity acknowledging that when the Father receives our worship, he receives it in the person of his Son and in the power of the Holy Spirit. I'd like to challenge worship leaders to be intentional in selecting songs that recognize the Trinity. Whether it is all three persons mentioned within one song, or three different songs, one for each person of the Godhead, the important thing is that we acknowledge Father, Son, and Holy Spirit within our gathered times of worship.

In addition, the songs sung in church worship services too often lack theological depth and instead feed our narcissistic tendencies. In these circumstances, secular culture has infected sacred worship evidenced by lyrics that focus more on who we are, what we have done, and how we interpret God and his actions, rather than on who God is, what he has done, and how Scripture reveals him to the world. This is especially troubling when we sing songs that portray an inaccurate image of God, or songs that use words and phrases that are contrary to what we know of God according to the Scriptures. When we sing lyrics that do not accurately image God and portray his actions, based on what we know of him through his word and centuries of orthodox Christian practice, we do not fulfill Jesus's desire for spirit and *truth* worship. In fact, I would suggest that when we sing songs that portray an inaccurate image of God, we are actually guilty of breaking the second commandment: "You shall not make for yourself an image in the form of anything in heaven above or on earth beneath or in the waters below . . . For I, the Lord your God, am a jealous God" (Exod 20:4–5, NIV).[19]

Selecting spiritually formative songs goes beyond avoiding heresy expressed within songs. We need to select songs that exalt the fullness of who God is and his story rather than songs that are simply "okay" or "good enough." Almighty God deserves much more than "just okay" songs. Leaders of congregational song must ask what a song says about God, how it speaks of God, and whether or not the song proclaims the truth of God as found in Scripture—allowing the congregation to respond to that truth in heartfelt, intellectual, and spiritually formative ways.

But what about making our worship services relevant to today's worshipers? Shouldn't we use songs that help those in attendance feel

---

19. When we read this command, some of us may quickly respond that we are not guilty of carving images and worshiping them. What we don't realize is that when we fail to project an accurate image of God as he has revealed himself in Scripture, we are guilty of creating a false image of God and breaking the second commandment.

comfortable in the worship service? Isn't it good to be sensitive to those seeking God by offering familiarity in the church gathering? These are some of the statements I regularly hear as a defense for using secular songs in worship services. We must first return to the purpose of the gathering. As discussed in the previous chapter, the purpose of the gathering is for worship, not evangelism. The body of Christ gathers together to proclaim the truth of God and respond to that truth. We gather for worship and scatter for evangelism. In other words, we gather as the body of Christ to re-spond to God's revelations and offer him worship that honors and glorifies his name, and then leave from there on our purposeful mission to tell oth-ers about Jesus. The issue and confusion in this area has occurred because we have misrepresented evangelism by implying that inviting someone to church is evangelism. But that is not evangelism, that is hospitality. Evan-gelism is telling others about Jesus Christ and the salvation offered through his life, death, and resurrection. Inviting someone to church so someone else can share the gospel (usually the trained, and paid, pastor) is not true evangelism. As a result, we have turned our times of gathered worship, the worship service, into an evangelism event. This has led to what was called the "seeker-sensitive" or "seeker-friendly" service.

The worship service is most definitely not intended for the unbe-liever, nonetheless this is not to say we should be unaware of those in the worship service who do not already have a relationship with God. Instead of "seeker-sensitive" or "seeker-friendly" gatherings, we should offer worship services that are "seeker-aware," understanding there may be unbelievers present and because of the worship of those who know God the Father, and have a relationship based on the work of his Son, those unbelievers will be drawn to God the Father, in the name of Jesus, through the power of the Holy Spirit. If we agree that worship songs form us spiritually, and that the purpose of the gathering is to worship God, then what would be the purpose in using secular songs in the worship service? The excuse of wanting the worship service to be relevant to un-believers isn't valid since Scripture and the truths of God are timeless and always relevant. Simone Weil states, "To be always relevant, you have to say things which are eternal."[20] Utilizing secular songs by secular art-ists such as Michael Jackson, Bon Jovi, the Beatles, Coldplay, or Adele in a worship service (each of which I have heard performed in church worship services) does not proclaim the truth of God and encourage the

20. Weil, quoted in Guinness, *No God but God*, 169.

congregation to respond to who God is. For the most part, the reason an unbeliever is sitting in a church worship service is because they are not finding what they need out in the world. They realize something is missing in their life so they go to church for help in discovering the missing piece of the puzzle. Why then would we offer them the world (secular songs) when they come to church? Let's give them something they can't find out in the world—the gathering of worshipers exalting the name of Jesus through song, prayer, etc.[21]

Allow me to share one more story in relation to this topic. When Pharrell Williams's song "Happy"[22] was released in 2013, I heard of at least five different churches that used the song in their worship services. Some used it as a presentational song, while others encouraged the congregation to sing along. I agree this is an irresistibly catchy song. My son's third-grade class performed it in a school assembly and it was enjoyable, mostly because of its catchy tune, not to mention twenty-five eight-year-old boys and girls singing and dancing. But here's the issue I have with using it in a worship service at church. Do you remember the lyrics of the song? Let's consider the chorus.

If we take the chorus line by line, we begin to see the problematic nature of using this song in a worship service. First we see the lyrics communicate that we are happy because we feel like a room without a roof. I'm not exactly sure what that means, but one possible explanation is that there are no limitations placed upon us—the sky's the limit. I'm not sure Scripture supports that notion, but let's move on. Next we notice the author pronounces that happiness is the truth. Wait . . . did we read that correctly? Yes—"happiness is the truth." This should be problematic for Christ-followers because Jesus is very clear in Scripture that he is the Way, the TRUTH, and the Life (John 14:6). Jesus is the truth, not happiness. Moving on to the third line, we are told to clap along if you know what happiness is to you.

---

21. When I say "the worship service is most definitely not intended for the unbeliever," I am not speaking of whether we should welcome unbelievers to our worship services. We should, of course, welcome all people to our worship services. That is being hospitable, a character trait that every Christian should practice superfluously. When I make the above statement, I am speaking from a planning perspective. Since the purpose of a worship service is for believers to gather to offer right response to God's revelations, the worship service should be planned accordingly, keeping in mind that some elements within the service may need to be explained or communicated in a particular way because unbelievers will be present (i.e., communion, or theological terms in songs and the sermon, etc.).

22. "Happy," words and music by Pharrell Williams © 2013 EMI Music Publishing

So the songwriter has told us that happiness is the truth and now is saying the truth ("happiness" to the songwriter) is relative—what is your truth? Again, as Christ-followers we know that truth is not relative. It is absolute. The truth is the truth. It does not change, it does not sway, it is steadfast, because Jesus, the Truth, is steadfast. Finally, the song tells us to clap along if we feel like that's what we wanna do. In other words, our response depends upon how we feel and therefore is optional. Yet as followers of Christ, our response to God, our worship, is not optional. We are commanded to respond through acts of worship. So, when we take a critical look at the song, and truly consider the lyrics, it becomes clear that this song is inappropriate to use in a worship service.[23]

Throughout Scripture, Christians are called to worship God in the manner that he prescribes, and not according to the shifting desires and changing fads of the unbelieving culture. If we worship according to God's truth and in his Spirit, the object of our worship will inevitably be God himself. In other words, our worship will be God-centered. To make anything other than God the center of our worship is idolatry. This is exceptionally serious and something we need to be concerned about in our worship services.

In case we believe we are safe because we would never think of using "secular songs" in our worship services, we must also thoughtfully consider the songs of worship that are intended to lead us in responding to God's revelations. There is potential for worship leaders to choose songs for congregational worship based on popularity or personal preference, yet the popularity of a song does not determine its quality or theological accuracy. There are songs currently being sung in churches that should be reconsidered due to the lyrical content being of questionable nature, as well as quality songs, filled with solid theological content, that are not being sung in many churches, but should be.

As leaders of sung praise, we must analyze and thoughtfully consider every worship song chosen for a worship service.[24] We must reclaim

23. I do not have a problem with Pharrell Williams. Mr. Williams did not write the song to be a Christian worship song performed in church. I do however, want to encourage church leaders to be more thoughtful in their selection of songs for use within worship services.

24. I encourage you to utilize some sort of rubric when considering songs to be used in a worship service. You can check out Cherry et al., *Selecting Worship Songs*, which includes a rubric for song evaluation. Or I highly recommend www.worshipbetter.com. Worship Better draws on well-established principles from the field of worship studies

our songs for the glory of God—Father, Son, and Holy Spirit—and his story. God has been at work in history, from biblical times to recent years to create a plethora of solid, gospel-rich, doctrinally faithful, Christ-exalting, songs. We must protect against songs that appear theologically skewed and that may mislead our people. As we have seen, the songs we sing form us spiritually so we must be sure to sing songs with biblical truths and theological depth—that tell God's story of creation, incarnation, and re-creation.

CONSIDER THIS

Take a look at the song database of your church. Make a list of which songs mention the Trinity, those that mention only God the Father, those that mention Jesus, and those that only mention the Holy Spirit. Determine whether you feel as though your church would benefit from a more balanced song list. If so, search for songs that mention the person of the Godhead in which your song database lacks or songs that mention all three in one song.

Try composing lyrics that name all three persons of the Trinity. If you are a musician, try composing a tune to go along with those lyrics. If you are not a musician, select a sing-able hymn and place your new lyrics within the hymn tune.

FOR FURTHER CONSIDERATION

Begbie, Jeremy S. *Theology, Music and Time*. Cambridge: Cambridge University Press, 2000.

Best, Harold M. *Music Through the Eyes of Faith*. San Francisco: Christian College Coalition, 1993.

Bradley, C. Randall. *From Memory to Imagination: Reforming the Church's Music*. Grand Rapids: Eerdmans, 2012.

Cherry, Constance. *The Music Architect: Blueprints for Engaging Worshipers in Song*. Grand Rapids: Baker Academic, 2016.

Ingalls, Monique. *Singing the Congregation: Contemporary Worship Music Forms Evangelical Community*. New York: Oxford University Press, 2018.

Kidd, Reggie M. *With One Voice: Discovering Christ's Song in Our Worship*. Grand Rapids: Baker, 2005.

Westermeyer, Paul. *The Heart of the Matter: Church Music as Praise, Prayer, Proclamation, Story and Gift*. Chicago: GIA, 2001.

---

and gives you a user-friendly, online tool for considering your songs' faith-formative impact.

3

Prayer as an Act of Worship

First of all, then, I urge that supplications, prayers, intercessions, and thanksgivings be made for all people, for kings and all who are in high positions, that we may lead a peaceful and quiet life, godly and dignified in every way. This is good, and it is pleasing in the sight of God our Savior, who desires all people to be saved and to come to the knowledge of the truth.

—1 Timothy 2:1–4

The planning of prayer as an essential component of a worship service takes time and effort. That statement may seem obvious and most people would probably agree that prayer should be a significant part of any worship service. However, in many modern evangelical churches, prayer is oftentimes an afterthought when it comes to the planning and programming of a service. I believe Scripture and prayer are the foundation for any worship service and should be treated as such. Without laying the foundation properly, you could end up with a disaster on your hands.

When I plan a worship service, I purposely plan the service with a reading of Scripture near the beginning in order to embed the word of God upon the minds, lips, and hearts of the congregation from the start. There are different ways to implement this reading: the worship leader may read the passage of Scripture as a solo voice; it may be presented as a responsive reading; it could be read in unison by the entire congregation; or any number of other possibilities. From week to week, I generally use multiple formats for the reading of Scripture, including the passage that opens the service. Following the opening Scripture reading I will often lead the congregation in the first song. This song may serve as an extension of the call to worship. It is a song that declares the attributes of God and informs the worshiper of God's presence. In other words, it is a song about God.

Following the first song, I offer a prayer in response to what we've just heard from God through the Scripture reading and song. In doing this, I've established Scripture and prayer as the foundation of the service. We have heard from God (his revelation) and can now proceed with other worship elements (our response) throughout the remainder of our time together. There will, of course, be other revelations from God during the service—additional Scripture readings, the sermon, etc.—nevertheless, I want to be sure that we begin the service with a revelation from God in order to encourage an appropriate response.

There are additional ways to offer opportunities for prayer within a worship service. At one church in which I served, we had a moment in the worship service for a focused time of prayer. During a designated song the congregation was invited to approach members of a prayer team for prayer. These prayer leaders were interspersed throughout the sanctuary—at the front, on the sides, and in the back. Every week, people were given the opportunity to approach the prayer leaders to receive prayer, blessings, and encouragement. The prayer leaders would pray with individuals, couples, and families. At times, especially when difficult circumstances surrounded one's life, a whole group of people—family, friends, loved ones—gathered together to pray for one another. During this time, prayer not only occurred with the prayer leaders, but within the congregation. Friends and family would turn to one another at their seats and would pray together. This focused time in the service was a wonderful act of worship as the congregation prayed together.

It is important for us to plan various times of prayer in our worship services. I know there are some who do not believe in planning prayer or using pre-scripted prayers in worship. However, I must wonder why worship leaders spend hours preparing songs for the worship service but no time preparing prayers? Something as important as leading others in communicating with the God of the universe should necessitate preparation. Of course there are times when special moments of prayer occur spontaneously. We should always be open to the moving of the Holy Spirit in any given situation. Yet planned times of worship, which includes prayer, are needed. In fact, it is in these purposeful times of prayer that we model for the congregation how to live a lifestyle of worship-filled dedication to the Lord.

Furthermore, as we consider preparing prayers for worship, it has always been interesting to me that we view using songs in our worship services that someone else wrote as acceptable, but struggle with using prayers that someone else wrote. There are many meaningful prayers written for public, corporate use, by men and women of God throughout history, as well as prayers that come to us from around the globe, that have the potential of leading and encouraging us in our worship. I would urge worship leaders to consider utilizing these prayers as a means of assisting the congregation in worship.

❖ ❖ ❖

It has been stated previously that within our worship, we declare and enact God's story of creation, incarnation, and re-creation. In addition, it can be said, worship prays God's story. Because of our redemption found in Christ, and by the means of praise and thanksgiving, public prayer ushers all of creation to the Father through Jesus Christ by the Spirit. Throughout the history of the church, it is evident that worship not only contains prayer, but is the prayer of the church for the life of the world and is the foundation for the wellbeing and salvation of all its inhabitants.

We observe solid content of public prayers throughout Scripture as well as in ancient documents such as the Didache from the early part of the second century. Spontaneous prayers are also valuable and their usage is encouraged—including in the ancient writings. An area of consideration when it comes to spontaneous prayers is the concern for the lack of content often found within these prayers. Too often, spontaneous prayers are delivered in a weak manner and as a transitional element in the worship service. However, prayer is spiritually formative so we must pay attention to the content and quality of our prayers, whether they are prepared in advance or offered spontaneously.

Some consider the Puritans masters at prayer. They subjected themselves to the intense discipline of private prayer, and were well-prepared and enthusiastic in public prayer. Richard Mather, one of the earliest ministers of the Massachusetts Bay Colony, was well-known for his discipline of prayer. Each day he conducted morning and evening prayer with his family, in addition to spending time alone in his prayer closet. On Sundays, his public prayers were highly respected by his congregation. At times, they lasted almost as long as the sermon.

William Perkins, a distinguished Puritan theologian of the late sixteenth century, taught that the Christian minister, like the prophets of ancient Israel, had two functions. First was the preaching and teaching of the word of God; and second, presenting the needs of the people before their God. Perkins preferred to show the importance of the prayer ministry of such men as Moses, Elijah, and Jeremiah. Perkins thought of prayer as a prophetic ministry that demanded the same gifts of discernment and inspiration that preaching demanded.[25]

In our modern worship services, do we consider the spiritually formative impact of prayer upon our lives and the lives of the congregation? For those that lead in worship, thoughtfulness with the words we choose for prayer is critically important. We must speak words that honor and glorify God, and proclaim truth because the congregation is formed in spiritual ways as a result of the prayers in the worship service. Worship service leaders must be conscientious so as to not end up in a situation similar to that which is portrayed in the following satirical article:

> During a brief prayer while leading worship at Tidal Wave Church Sunday morning, local worship leader Brian "Hatchback" Lancer managed to espouse no less than 47 different heresies, according to witnesses.
>
> "Father God, we just come before Your Spirit now and we just thank You, Father God, for dying on the cross for us," Lancer's prayer began, immediately falling into heresy. "Send the Father down in power now, and let Your Son fill this place as we glorify the Spirit now, Lord Jesus."
>
> "Thanks so much, Daddy, for creating Jesus and sending him to earth in spirit so we could learn to fulfill your law, Holy Spirit," he continued.
>
> As his fellow Christians could only peek out one eye and watch in terror, Lancer plowed forward, totally unaware he was totally botching nearly every facet of Christian thought, repeating a long parade of heresies from throughout church history. In the brief, whimsical prayer, Lancer managed to stumble into Gnosticism, Pelagianism, Arianism, Patripassionism, and a brand-new heresy with elements of both modalism and the plot of Stargate SG-1.

25. Old, *Leading in Prayer*, 5–6.

"It was pretty amazing, actually," said head pastor Matt Wetzel. "I was going to stop him, but I wanted to see if he could hit every apostasy known to man." Wetzel also admitted he needs to do a better job shepherding the worship leader. "Yeah, I guess that's my job, isn't it?"[26]

Prayer that contains biblical truth and sound orthodoxy spiritually forms worshipers in significant ways. Another way to say it is good prayer forms us well while bad prayer poorly forms us.

In pubic worship, there are three types of prayer the worship leader can employ: fixed prayers, spontaneous prayers, and extemporaneous prayers. Fixed prayers are those prayers that have been written prior to the worship service. These may be original prayers written by the worship leader or prayers written by someone else at a different time and place. Prayers found in the Book of Common Prayer would be an example of a fixed prayer. There are many benefits to utilizing fixed prayers. A fixed prayer offers the opportunity to present a thoroughly thought-out prayer to God on behalf of the people. If the worship leader is going to encourage corporate praying, a fixed prayer is a good option as you can place the prayer in the bulletin or on the screen. Fixed prayers are also beneficial in teaching people how to pray in public. By writing out the prayer, the prayer may be rehearsed in advance in an attempt to become comfortable with the words before delivering the prayer in front of the group.

The downside of utilizing fixed prayers is that they may fall flat if the person praying does not speak the prayer with fervor and sincerity. Fixed prayers may also encourage formalism and stifle spontaneity, and can lack variety and applicability to many modern situations. In utilizing fixed prayers, with the understanding that prayer spiritually forms the worshiper, one must prepare to deliver the prayer well, just as one would prepare a song or sermon.

Here is a fixed prayer by Charles Spurgeon that may be used in corporate worship:

> Our precious Lord Jesus Christ, we adore you with all our hearts. You are Lord of all, and we bless you for becoming man so that you could become our next of kin, and being next of kin we bless you for taking us into marriage union with yourself and for redeeming us from the captivity into which we were sold. You have paid

26. The Babylon Bee, "Worship Leader Commits 47 Heresies In 30–Second Prayer," October 18, 2018.

your life to make us family, we have been ransomed with your own heart's blood. And as a result may you forever be loved and adored. Even now you are seated on your throne in heaven as you reign over all things, as the never-ending song "worthy is the lamb" sounds to give you the praise and glory that you alone deserve. And we say "Amen" this morning. From the outskirts of the crowd that surrounds your throne we lift up our feeble voice in earnest, for you were slain and have redeemed us to God, and we shall reign with you forever. Awaken us to all that we have in Christ, reminding us of what you have done, and the privilege that is ours to be your representatives here on earth. Jesus, we praise you and honor you as our Lord and Savior. Amen.

Here is another fixed prayer for public corporate worship, from the Book of Common Prayer, to be prayed on All Saints Day:[27]

Almighty God, who hast knit together thine elect in one communion and fellowship in the mystical body of Your Son, Christ our Lord: Give us grace so to follow Your blessed saints in all virtuous and godly living, that we may come to those ineffable joys that thou hast prepared for those who unfeignedly love thee; through the same Jesus Christ our Lord, who with thee and the Holy Spirit liveth and reigneth, one God, in glory everlasting. Amen.

Spontaneous prayers are those given on the spot without any preparation. Many times these prayers are offered "on the fly" without much thought given to them, including during the prayer. Because of the lack of preparation, oftentimes "spontaneous" prayers can become predictable and routine as the person praying reverts back to familiar phrases and generic spiritual statements. In addition, the person praying may express quite theologically unsound sentiments, or give way to sentimentality or to shear verbosity. These are the downsides of spontaneous prayers. There are, however, benefits to spontaneous prayers. There are times when the Holy Spirit moves within a worship service and the most appropriate response at that moment is to pray. It may not be planned, but it is the right thing to do at that moment.

---

27. For my Protestant friends who may not be familiar with this day, All Saints' Day is a special day in the Christian Year (November 1) providing an opportunity for the church to acknowledge those who have gone before and set an example for us in the faith. Think about the person who shared Jesus with you when you accepted him as your personal Lord and Savior. What about the person who shared Jesus with them. How valuable are these people in the line of those who have gone before leaving a legacy of faith for you to follow? All Saints Day provides an opportunity to give thanks for those who have mentored, guided, and blazed a path for us in the faith.

Extemporaneous prayers are given extemporaneously after minimal preparation. Definitions of extemporaneous include "carried out or performed with little or no preparation" and "prepared in advance but delivered without notes or text." These prayers are not read from a page, such as most fixed prayers, yet are thought through in advance, unlike spontaneous prayers. For example, I may put together a worship service that begins with the song "Holy, Holy, Holy, Lord God Almighty" and then proceeds to the song "Holy Is the Lord." As I am planning the service, I know I want to pray between the two songs, so I prepare bullet points (either on paper or in my mind) for the prayer:

- Open by naming God as holy

- Praise God for what he has done, is doing, and is yet to do

- Thank God for the opportunity to be gathered together to worship

- Assert the words of Isaiah (chapter 6) "Holy, holy, holy . . . "

- Trinitarian closing—Father, Son, and Holy Spirit

Although the outline for my prayer has been thoughtfully considered ahead of time, when I pray the prayer in public worship, I simply expand upon each bullet point throughout the prayer.

The benefit of extemporaneous praying is that although it is prepared in advance, it still has the feeling of being casual and somewhat spontaneous. The downside depends on how much preparation was made. If adequate preparation does not occur, an extemporaneous prayer can easily lead to rambling.

Each of these three types of prayer are acceptable forms of praying in the church. We see each type in Scripture as well as throughout church history. We can only suppose that Jesus and the apostles were brought up with a fair measure of liturgy in the Jewish traditions. We know they would have prayed fixed prayers on a regular basis within public worship at the temple and synagogue. Yet, there are clearly spontaneous and extemporary prayers offered from time to time. There would seem to be room for both. What is important is that prayer, whether read or extemporized, should be biblical and reflect a true understanding of God.

There are a variety of prayers that can be offered in public worship; each possessing a different function and, when utilized well, serve to aide in the spiritual formation of the participant.[28]

28. I recommend *Leading in Prayer: A Workbook for Worship* by Hughes Oliphant

INVOCATION

The purpose of an invocation prayer is not to invite God, who is elsewhere, to come be part of the gathered worship—for we know that God is present everywhere at all times (Ps 139:7–12). It is intended rather to remind those gathered of whom they have come to worship while declaring to God that the congregation is willing and available for him to work within each person. It is an opportunity for the assembly to be open to what God would like to do in their midst as they gather for worship. The invocation prayer generally occurs at or near the beginning of the worship service to set the tone for the congregation's focus on God.

Examples

Invocation 1

O Lord, from the rising of the sun to the setting of the same, your name is to be praised.

Merciful God, gracious Lord, Sovereign One:

Hear us in the name of your Son who has promised that where two or three are gathered in his name he would be with us. Moreover, he promised that our prayers would be heard.

Hear us in the name of your Son. For he is the revelation of your wisdom, the outpouring of your glory, the incarnation of your mercy, not only toward us, but to the whole human race.

To you be glory, all praise and honor, you who are Three in One, Father, Son, and Holy Spirit, now and evermore. Amen.

Invocation 2

Lord, we come into your house this morning to praise your faithfulness, give thanks for your mercy, and seek your joy. Thank you for creating us and giving us life and breath today. Thank you for your Son Jesus Christ, our Savior and for the Holy Spirit whose presence here unites us as your people. Fill us with your peace today. Amen.

Old if you would like to learn more about the various types of prayers listed here, or if you would like to have resources for leading corporate prayer.

THE PSALMS

Praying the Psalms together has been a long-standing tradition in Christian worship over the centuries. The Psalms are wonderful resources appropriate for use as prayers. Many of the Psalms deal specifically with life circumstances and heartfelt emotions. Some of the Psalms are personal and intimate, while others are appropriate for use in congregational worship. Using the Psalms in corporate worship will shape your church's thinking about God, man, the world, and how we respond to it all.

Examples

Psalm 139:23–24

"Search me, O God, and know my heart; test me and know my anxious thoughts. See if there is any offensive way in me, and lead me in the way everlasting."

Psalm 51:1–4a; 17

"Be gracious to me, O God, according to Your loving-kindness; According to the greatness of Your compassion blot out my transgressions. Wash me thoroughly from my iniquity and cleanse me from my sin. For I know my transgressions, and my sin is ever before me. Against You, You only, I have sinned and done what is evil in Your sight. My sacrifice, O God, is a broken spirit; a broken and contrite heart you, God, will not despise."

Psalm 63:1–2

"O God, you are my God, earnestly I seek you; my soul thirsts for you, my body longs for you, in a dry and weary land where there is no water. I have seen you in the sanctuary and beheld your power and your glory. Because your love is better than life, my lips will glorify you."

CONFESSION

The purpose of the confession prayer is to offer the congregation an opportunity to confess sins to God, asking for his complete and absolute forgiveness. This is a vital part of Christian worship and one that is too often neglected in many Protestant worship gatherings. Prayers of confession provide opportunities to share our deepest weaknesses and failures with God and others that we trust, so we may enter into God's grace and mercy and experience his ready forgiveness and healing. The importance of confession is even modeled for us in the prayer of Jesus when he teaches his disciples; "forgive us our debts." When we request forgiveness from God through a prayer of confession, we invite God to renew his relationship with us and to restore us to walking closely with him.

Example

O Lord, merciful Father, have mercy on us, for we are sinners.
We confess that things have fallen apart and we need your restoration. We are so prone to wander from you and your truth.
O Lord, you remain faithful even when we are unfaithful.
Your steadfast love remains even when we neglect to love.
By your Holy Spirit restore our souls that we might show your love and share your truth with the world.
O Lord, merciful Father, hear our prayers in the name of your Son, Jesus Christ, to whom be glory for ever and ever. Amen.

After the prayer of confession, it is appropriate to offer what's called an assurance of pardon. This is an important part of confession, as the congregation needs to be reminded, or assured, that God has forgiven all confessed sin:

Example (from 1 John 1:5, 7, 9; 2:1–2)

"This is the message we have heard from him and proclaim to you, that God is light and in him is no darkness at all. . . . If we walk in the light, as he is in the light, we have fellowship with one another, and the blood of Jesus his Son cleanses us from all sin. . . . If we confess our sins, he is faithful and just, and will forgive our sins and cleanse us from all unrighteousness. . . . We have an advocate with the Father, Jesus Christ the righteous; and he is the expiation for our sins, and not for ours only but also for the sins of the whole world."

ILLUMINATION

The prayer of illumination asks God to provide an opportunity for us to experience him in our worship. In some churches, the illumination prayer is prayed immediately preceding the sermon. This prayer asks God to open our eyes to see what he would have us see, to open our ears to hear what he would have us hear, and to open our minds to understand what he would desire for us to understand. This is similar to what the apostle Paul prayed for the church of Ephesus:

> . . . that the God of our Lord Jesus Christ, the Father of glory, may give you the Spirit of wisdom and of revelation in the knowledge of him, having the eyes of your hearts enlightened, that you may know what is the hope to which he has called you, what are the riches of his glorious inheritance in the saints, and what is the immeasurable greatness of his power toward us who believe, according to the working of his great might. (Eph 1:17–19)

As we have seen earlier, when we see God for who he is, we are changed.

Example

O Lord, as we gather together in your name, enlighten our hearts that we may see you; enlighten our hearts that we may hear you; enlighten our hearts that we may know you more.

O Father, our hope is found in you and you alone. Lead us in your righteousness and may your Spirit guide us to life everlasting through your Son, Jesus Christ.

For it is in his name that we pray, now and forevermore. Amen.

INTERCESSION

Prayers of intercession are a major element of public worship in the Christian church. It is in these intercessory prayers that we continue the ministry that Jesus gave to the church as we intercede on behalf of others. We pray as a community, for the community, and for the concerns of the community. Praying for others can deepen your faith and enhance your life. Yet that is not the purpose of intercessory prayer. We pray for others because prayer actually does help people. As the people of God, we must believe that prayer works. Additionally, praying for others increases our love for them, helping us fulfill the second part of the great command to "love your neighbor as yourself." Furthermore, since Christians are imitators of Christ, we should follow Jesus's example of intercessory praying:

> I do not ask for these only, but also for those who will believe in me through their word, that they may all be one, just as you, Father, are in me, and I in you, that they also may be in us, so that the world may believe that you have sent me. The glory that you have given me I have given to them, that they may be one even as we are one, I in them and you in me, that they may become perfectly one, so that the world may know that you sent me and loved them even as you loved me. (John 17:20–23)

Example

Almighty Father, O Lord of Zion, whose name is great among the nations, we lift up our hands in the name of Jesus, offering up our prayers on every shore to you, O Father, to whom praise is ever due.

Father, we pray for the church, that she might be prepared for her Bride, adorned for her husband. Give to her true purity, that she might be without spot or wrinkle. Give her the grace of hope and the confidence of joy, as she awaits the coming of the Bridegroom.

We pray for own congregation. Grant that it might be a sign here on earth of the church that is above.

Father, we pray for those who lead our church, for pastors, for elders, for deacons. Fill them with the Spirit of wisdom and understanding, the Spirit of counsel and might, the Spirit of knowledge and of fear of the Lord.

Father, whose love and concern is for a world filled with a great variety of people, we pray for people in different lands, for Mexicans and Brazilians and Colombians; for Watsui, Masai, Ibu, and all the tribes of Africa; for all peoples in China, Malaysia, and Indonesia; for French people and English people, Greeks and Russians. Grant that the gospel might be heard in all the corners of the earth.

Father, we pray for those who lead our nation. Anoint them with the gifts of your Spirit, honesty, fairness, and intelligence; love, and peace, and learning.

Father and Shepherd of the flock of your people, we pray for the members of our congregation, for husbands and wives, that their love for each other might be ever richer and kinder, for children and young people, that they might grow in every good direction, for people who live alone, that they might find friendship and community,

For grandparents and elderly friends, that they might have that radiance which belongs to older years.

All these mercies we ask in the name of Jesus, who ever sits at your right hand, O Father. He it is who is our intercessor, and it is through him that we are taught to pray, saying,

Our Father in heaven, hallowed be your name. Your kingdom come, your will be done, on earth as it is in heaven. Give us this day our daily bread, and forgive us our debts as we also have forgiven our debtors. And lead us not into temptation, but deliver us from evil. For yours is the kingdom, the power and the glory, forever and ever. Amen.

COMMUNION

The purpose of the communion prayer is to bless and thank God for his ultimate sacrifice on the cross for our sins. Throughout the history of the church, there have been various prayers for communion, based on Scripture and traditions. The three general prayers include the Communion Invocation offered at the beginning of communion; the Eucharistic Prayer over the bread and the cup; and a Post-Communion Thanksgiving at the end to give thanks for the grace received at the Table and offering dedicated service to Christ's kingdom work.

Examples

Communion Invocation
(prayer before distribution of communion elements)[29]

Most merciful Lord, your love compels us to come in. Our hands were unclean, our hearts were unprepared; we were not fit even to eat the crumbs from under your table. But you, Lord, are the God of our salvation, and share your bread with sinners. So cleanse and feed us with the precious body and blood of your Son, that he may live in us and we in him; and that we, with the whole company of Christ, may sit and eat in your kingdom. Amen.

---

29. Cited in Church of England, *Common Worship*.

The Great Thanksgiving (congregational response in italics)[30]

The Lord be with you. *And also with you.*
Lift up your hearts. *We lift them up to the Lord.*
Let us give thanks to the Lord our God. *It is right to give our thanks and praise.*

It is right, and a good and joyful thing, always and everywhere to give thanks to you, Father Almighty, creator of heaven and earth. You formed us in your image and breathed into us the breath of life. When we turned away, and our love failed, your love remained steadfast. You delivered us from captivity, made covenant to be our sovereign God, and spoke to us from your prophets. And so, with your people on earth and all the company of heaven we praise your name and join their unending hymn:
Holy, holy, holy Lord, God of power and might,
heaven and earth are full of your glory. Hosanna in the highest.
Blessed is he who comes in the name of the Lord. Hosanna in the highest.

Holy are you, and blessed is your Son Jesus Christ. Your Spirit anointed him to preach good news to the poor, to proclaim release to the captive and recovering of sight to the blind, to set at liberty those who are oppressed, and announce that the time had come when you would save your people. He healed the sick, fed the hungry, and ate with sinners. By the baptism of his suffering, death, and resurrection you gave birth to your church, delivered us from slavery to sin and death, and made with us a new covenant by water and the Spirit. When the Lord Jesus ascended, he promised to be with us always, in the power of your word and Holy Spirit.

On the night in which he gave himself up for us, he took bread, gave thanks to you, broke the bread, gave it to his disciples, and said: "Take, eat; this is my body which is given to you. Do this in remembrance of me." When the supper was over, he took the cup, gave thanks to you, gave it to his disciples, and said: "Drink from this, all of you; this is my blood of the new covenant, poured out for you and for many for the forgiveness of sins. Do this, as often as you drink it, in remembrance of me."

---

30. This prayer, the Great Thanksgiving, follows ancient patterns of prayer, both Jewish and Christian, by filling the prayer with commemoration of God's activity. Compare 1 Kings 8:15–21, Acts 4:24–30, or Ephesians 1:3–18, among many possible examples. In special feasts and seasons, variations of the prayer will pick up the appropriate tone and themes of the church calendar.

And so, in remembrance of this your mighty acts in Jesus Christ, we offer ourselves in praise and thanksgiving as a holy and living sacrifice, in union with Christ's offering for us, as we proclaim the mystery of faith:
Christ has died; Christ is risen; Christ will come again.
Pour out your Holy Spirit on us gathered here, and on these gifts of bread and wine. Make them be for us the body and blood of Christ that we may be for the world the body of Christ, redeemed by his blood. By your Spirit make us one with Christ, one with each other, and one in ministry to all the world until Christ comes in final victory and we feast at his heavenly banquet. Through your Son Jesus Christ, with the Holy Spirit in your holy church, all honor and glory is yours, almighty Father now and forever. *Amen.*

Communion Thanksgiving Prayer
(prayer after distribution of communion elements)[31]

Father of all, we give you thanks and praise, that when we were still far off you met us in your Son and brought us home. Dying and living, he declared your love, gave us grace, and opened the gate of glory. May we who share Christ's body live his risen life; we who drink his cup bring life to others; we whom the Spirit lights give light to the world. Keep us firm in the hope you have set before us, so we and all your children shall be free, and the whole earth live to praise your name; through Christ our Lord. Amen.

THANKSGIVING

Thanksgiving prayers acknowledge that God has blessed us. We thereby offer thanks to God for all he has done, is doing, and will do in the time to come. The Bible is clear that we should practice giving thanks to God regularly, showing him our gratitude for all he does for us, and acknowledging that he provides everything we need for our lives (Ps 106:1; 107:1; 118:1; 1 Chr 16:34; 1 Thess 5:18). Being thankful requires a person to turn away from self-focus and become other-focused. Fifteenth-century German Dominican theologian Meister Eckhart once remarked, "If the only prayer you ever said in your whole life was 'thank you,' that would suffice." Practicing gratitude connects our heart to God and forms our inner being to see something bigger than ourselves. Gratitude sets a foundation for God to change us in profound ways.

31. Cited in *Common Worship.*

Examples

Paul's prayer found in his letter to the Ephesians is a wonderful example of a prayer of Thanksgiving:

> Blessed be the God and Father of our Lord Jesus Christ, who has blessed us in Christ with every spiritual blessing in the heavenly places, even as he chose us in him before the foundation of the world, that we should be holy and blameless before him. In love he predestined us for adoption as sons through Jesus Christ, according to the purpose of his will, to the praise of his glorious grace, with which he has blessed us in the Beloved. In him we have redemption through his blood, the forgiveness of our trespasses, according to the riches of his grace, which he lavished upon us, in all wisdom and insight making known to us the mystery of his will, according to his purpose, which he set forth in Christ as a plan for the fullness of time, to unite all things in him, things in heaven and things on earth. (Eph 1:3–10)

Here is a Thanksgiving prayer adapted from the preface to the Eucharistic Prayer, from the Divine Liturgy of Saint John Chrysostom:

> It is fitting and right to hymn you, to give you thanks, to worship you in all places of your dominion. For you are God, and we have no words to describe you adequately. We can't fully get our minds around you, and though we can't see you, or comprehend you, we know that you are unchanging, as the eternal Three-In-One, Father, Son, and Spirit.
>
> You brought us out of not-being; and when we had fallen, you raised us up again; and did not cease to do everything until you had brought us up to heaven, and granted us the kingdom that is to come. For all these things we give thanks to you and to your only-begotten Son and to your Holy Spirit, for all that we know and do not know, your seen and unseen benefits that have come upon us. We give you thanks also for this ministry of praise and worship from our lips, even though thousands of archangels and ten thousands of angels stand before you, cherubim and seraphim, with six wings and many eyes, flying on high singing the triumphal hymn proclaiming with a loud voice: "Holy, holy, holy, Lord God Almighty; heaven and earth are full of your glory. Hosanna in the highest. Blessed is he who comes in the name of the Lord. Hosanna in the highest.

BENEDICTION[32]

Offering a benediction at the end of a worship service is one of the oldest biblical worship traditions. Here are just a few benedictions found in the Bible that you can pronounce over your congregation.

Examples

Numbers 6:24–26

"The Lord bless you and keep you; the Lord make his face to shine upon you and be gracious to you; the Lord lift up his countenance upon you and give you peace."

Acts 20:32

"And now I commend you to God and to the word of his grace, which is able to build you up and to give you the inheritance among all those who are sanctified."

Romans 15:13

"May the God of hope fill you with all joy and peace in believing, so that by the power of the Holy Spirit you may abound in hope."

2 Corinthians 13:14

"The grace of the Lord Jesus Christ and the love of God and the fellowship of the Holy Spirit be with you all."

2 Thessalonians 2:16–17

"Now may our Lord Jesus Christ himself, and God our Father, who loved us and gave us eternal comfort and good hope through grace, comfort your hearts and establish them in every good work and word."

---

32. The benediction is God's good word to us, which is essentially what the word "benediction" means. It is a compound word from the Latin *bene*, which means "good," and *dicere*, which means "to speak." From that comes the Latin word *benedictio*, which means "blessing." It is a pronouncement of God's blessing upon his people.

DOXOLOGY

In American Protestant churches that utilize a benediction, a doxology often follows the benediction. A doxology is a short prayer or hymn of praise that extols the glory and majesty of God. Doxology simply means "glory" or "praise." There are many doxologies, although the one most often used is sung to the tune of "Old Hundredth" with words by Thomas Ken:

> Praise God from whom all blessings flow,
> Praise him all creatures here below,
> Praise him above ye heavenly hosts,
> Praise Father, Son, and Holy Ghost. Amen.

Biblical doxologies

Romans 16:27

"To the only wise God be glory forevermore through Jesus Christ! Amen."

Ephesians 3:20–21

"Now to him who is able to do far more abundantly than all that we ask or think, according to the power at work within us, to him be glory in the church and in Christ Jesus throughout all generations, forever and ever. Amen."

Jude 24 and 25

"Now to him who is able to keep you from stumbling and to present you blameless before the presence of his glory with great joy, to the only God, our Savior, through Jesus Christ our Lord, be glory, majesty, dominion, and authority, before all time and now and forever. Amen."

Liturgical doxologies

Gloria Patri

The Lesser Doxology, so called to distinguish it from the Greater Doxology, is also known as the *Gloria Patri*: "Glory be to the Father, and to the Son, and to the Holy Spirit; as it was in the beginning, is now, and ever shall be, world without end. Amen."

Gloria in Excelsis Deo

The Greater Doxology, known as the *Gloria in Excelsis Deo*, is an early church expansion of the song of the angels in Luke 2:14: "Glory to God in the highest, and on earth peace to people of good will. We praise you, we bless you, we adore you, we glorify you, we give you thanks for your great glory, Lord God, heavenly King, O God almighty Father.

Lord Jesus Christ, Only Begotten Son, Lord God, Lamb of God, Son of the Father, you take away the sins of the world, have mercy on us; you take away the sins of the world, receive our prayer; you are seated at the right hand of the Father, have mercy on us.

For You alone are the Holy One, you alone are the Lord, you alone are the Most High, Jesus Christ, with the Holy Spirit, in the glory of God the Father. Amen."

Trinitarian

There is a special doxology called the trinitarian doxology:

> "Through him, with him, in him, in the unity of the Holy Spirit,
> all glory and honor is yours, almighty Father, for ever and ever."

Regardless of the function, the ultimate purpose of each prayer is the same; to strengthen the worshiper's relationship with God. As we pray we join with God on the journey of him changing us from the inside out by the power of Christ working within. Harold Best states,

> Prayer is above all about who God is and what he wants. By praying in his name, we pray for his sake—not on his behalf, neither to rescue him nor to inform him. Rather, by being found in him in Christ, we pray in him, walking the paths of his completed work that we do not yet see completed. . . . Thus we pray by faith, which is the substance and the evidence of our praying. Informed fully by his Word, living by faith, rooted in love and buoyed by hope, our praying and outpouring are as indivisible as Spirit and truth.[33]

---

33. Best, *Unceasing Worship*, 99.

Our prayers shape that which we are, both on the inside and on the outside. Therefore it is vital for those who lead in prayer to do so with utmost thoughtfulness and zeal. Our worship prays God's story.

A question to ask before closing the chapter on the spiritually formative aspect of prayer is, do we value prayer as we should? Do church leaders and congregations understand the importance of prayer in their lives? Dr. Constance Cherry, Professor of Worship and Christian Ministries at Indiana Wesleyan University, engaged in a field study to determine the value of various worship elements in the life of the church. She visited thirty churches in four states over the course of sixteen months. As she sat in the thirty-one worship services encompassing nineteen different denominations, she timed each element of worship within the service. It's been said that if you want to know what a person values, just look at their checkbook and calendar. Our values are revealed not by what we say but by what we do. Where do we spend most of our time and the majority of our money? At the conclusion of Dr. Cherry's study, she compiled the findings and wrote an article entitled, "My House Shall Be Called a House of . . . Announcements."[34] What she found was that contemporary worship services spent more time communicating the announcements than they did in prayer. What a sad indictment on the church—one I believe must be remedied.

CONSIDER THIS

I once heard it said that, in the corporate setting, having one person pray while everyone else listens is like having one person sing while everyone listens. Try planning prayers that incorporate those within the congregation in various ways.

Based on the descriptions of the assorted prayers in this chapter, try writing prayers of your own for use in a worship service.

FOR FURTHER CONSIDERATION

Bennett, Arthur. *The Valley of Vision: A Collection of Puritan Prayers & Devotions*. Carlisle: The Banner of Truth Trust, 1975.

Old, Hughes Oliphant. *Leading in Prayer: A Workbook for Worship*. Grand Rapids: Eerdmans, 1995.

34. Cherry, "My House Shall Be Called," 2004.

4

Scripture Reading as an Act of Worship

For the word of God is living and active, sharper than any two-edged sword, piercing to the division of soul and of spirit, of joints and of marrow, and discerning the thoughts and intentions of the heart.

—HEBREWS 4:12

A NUMBER OF YEARS ago I was challenged with the idea to focus on a renewal of Scripture in Sunday worship. This idea began as I sat with a group of ministry colleagues and discussed their observations on the lack of Scripture being used in the worship services at their various churches. These were pastors and worship leaders saying that Scripture was not being used enough in their churches. They mentioned how the worship leader may read a couple verses in between songs and the preacher would usually read the passage at the beginning of the sermon, but that was all. After being stunned, and finding myself in agreement as I considered my own ministry context, I began to wonder, "If not in our churches, where?" If we are not utilizing Scripture in our churches, within the context of our worship services, where are we using it?

This realization was the beginning of an idea to develop a Scripture Presentation Team for the church where I was serving at the time. The team would attempt to resolve the issue of a lack of Scripture utilization; at least in our local worship setting.

The goal of the Scripture Presentation Team was to enhance the presentation of the word of God and develop a culture of Scripture reading and understanding within the church. The team met twice a month for prayer, Bible study, rehearsals, and training, culminating in the planning and scheduling of Scripture presentations. I worked with the senior pastor to determine which passages of Scripture the team would present and on which Sunday. The team would then meet to study the Scripture passages and discuss various ways in which the passages could be presented to, and with, the congregation.

On Sunday mornings, team members would present the selected Scripture passage through various dramatic and artistic forms including monologues, group presentations, tableaus, reader's theater, etc., during the morning worship services.

The result was encouraging. The congregation responded positively to the team's presentations of Scripture and the word of God was being placed on the ears, minds, and lips of the congregation. The hearing of Scripture began to have a profound effect upon the congregation as they gathered together to worship the Lord.

A number of years later I was in Ukraine to teach at a worship conference. In addition to my teaching sessions I was asked if I would be willing to organize Scripture presentations for each day of the three-day conference. With the help of conference staff, I gathered three groups to rehearse the Scripture passages that would be presented each morning of the conference. Every presentation was creatively unique, sometimes including musical elements, but every time including some sort of artistic expression. As with my own church, the presentation of Scripture in these creative ways was positively received and many at the conference sought me out to share how they intended to take this idea back to their local churches. Those who participated in the Scripture presentations, as well as the hearers of the word, commented on how presenting Scripture in these ways helped the word of God come alive for them. Thanks be to God for the word of the Lord.

❖ ❖ ❖

The use of Scripture is foundational in celebrating God in worship. The Bible has always been central to the life of the Christian church. The ancient Hebrew stories, songs, prophecies, and wisdom that permeated the Jewish world of Jesus's day profoundly shaped even Jesus himself as he lived on the earth. The earliest Christians explored the Scriptures in an attempt to understand what Almighty God had accomplished through Jesus, and as a result, they conducted their lives accordingly. Today, we continue to study the Scriptures to discover how to worship, and thus how to live.

From the very beginning Scripture has been given a prominent place in the church's worshiping life, indicating that it has been understood to not only be part of the church's thinking, but also part of the church's worship. Scripture is a foundational element of all Christian worship in that it reveals God to the worshiper—what he has done in the past, what he is doing in the present, and what he will do in the future—and shows us what the appropriate response should be as we worship in spirit and truth.

The use of the Psalms is at the heart of Christian worship in many traditions. It is often utilized to encourage the praise and worship of God, just as it did for the Jewish people themselves in years past. The reading of the gospel indicates the belief that the Bible continues to be both a central way in which God reveals himself to his people and in how they respond.

If the importance of the word is vital to Christ-followers, why has Scripture fallen from its once prominent place in the Christian life? Robert Webber claims,

> we are nourished in worship by Jesus Christ, who is the living Word disclosed to us in the Scriptures, the written Word of God. In spite of all the emphasis we evangelicals have placed on the importance of the Bible, there seems to be a crisis of the Word among us. Consider what two evangelical pastors have to say.
>
> Pastor Jason Snook comments, "How ironic that Protestantism in particular, has moved so far away from an emphasis on the Word from which it found its origin!" Pastor Dave Wiebe thinks we are in a time of "closing the book." He believes that "more and more people are choosing to endorse and follow beliefs that are not in the book or not based on the book; they are cultural and societal myths." If these comments are indicative of what is taking place in our worship, then there is clearly a need to rethink our approach to Scripture in worship.[1]

In a survey, 1,033 American pastors described their highest ministry competencies as scriptural knowledge (85 percent), teaching (83 percent), and preaching (81 percent).[2] As a result, the conclusion can be made that the Bible is important to the church, as it should be. In the average church, however, a different story is told of the congregation. The same study shows

1. Webber, *Ancient-Future Worship*, 113.
2. Barna, *Today's Pastors*, 70–71.

that most Christians can't recite at least five of the Ten Commandments, can't name the four Gospels, don't know that Jesus is the one who preached the Sermon on the Mount, and think "God helps those who help themselves" is actually a verse in the Bible.[3] The researcher concludes that "Lay members are abysmally ignorant of the basics of the Bible . . . no amount of Bible-based preaching, scriptural teaching or small-group meetings moves the congregation to a higher plane of Bible knowledge . . . Obviously the Bible is not a high priority in the lives of most people."[4]

Moreover, the Bible no longer seems to be important in our corporate worship gatherings. Whereas in the past corporate worship services were filled with Scripture recitations, including Old Testament, New Testament, Epistle, and Psalm readings, the average evangelical church rarely incorporates each of these today. We have seen a trend of more singing and longer sermons, resulting in less Scripture reading. Most often, Scripture is relegated to the sermon, and even then, many sermons today are moving away from exegetical and expository preaching (delving into the text for greater understanding) and moving to focusing on a biblical thought, sometimes offering just a self-help, inspirational type of message. The importance of Scripture is given lip service but is not given priority in many of our churches.

Harold Best speaks of the responsibility of the Christian in relation to Scripture. Best states that "Christians should be amateur theologians and Scripture specialists, but in the older meaning of the word. Amateurs are those who love something (hence the Latin *ama* at the beginning of the word) enough to study and practice it as thoroughly as possible, to become skilled in it, without the need to call it a profession or a specialized calling. The core of our being is the image of God, and the core of our spiritual being is in Christ."[5]

One constant of true worship is the word of God. This is seen throughout centuries of Christian worship, particularly in the covenant. Covenant between God and man is one of the greatest themes of the Bible. God makes a covenant with his people in order to reveal the relationship between Creator and his created ones, based on who God is and how we are to respond to him. Ultimately, covenant lies at the heart of true, authentic worship.

3. Barna, *Today's Pastors*, 48–49.
4. Barna, *Today's Pastors*, 48.
5. Best, *Unceasing Worship*, 67.

This covenant from God came primarily in two forms—oral and written. A very important transition occurred when Israel left Egypt. When they arrived at Sinai, the covenant was no longer to be transmitted strictly in an oral fashion, but it was to be passed on in written form as well. First, Moses conveyed God's covenant with his people orally, in which they wholeheartedly agreed—"Moses came and told the people all the words of the Lord and all the rules. And all the people answered with one voice and said, 'All the words that the Lord has spoken we will do'" (Exod 24:3). Next, a written summary of the covenant called the "Book of the Covenant" was compiled (Exod 24:4a). Then Moses, after returning from atop the mountain, presented two stone tablets to the people displaying the covenant written by the very "finger of God" (Exod 31:18).

The importance of Scripture was so important to Moses that his last directive before his death was for Joshua to offer a covenant renewal ceremony for the people of Israel. This was not a suggestion from Moses, but rather a command: "Moses and the elders of Israel commanded the people" (Deut 27:1). There was no getting around the fact that following God's word was not a suggestion. It was a directive. And Joshua obeyed, writing the covenant on the stones atop Mount Ebal followed by the reading of the entire Law, each and every word, to all the people.

It is important to note that the reading and recitation of Scripture took time. In the early years of the church, Justin Martyr (b.100–d.165) records that when the Christians would gather for worship, they would listen to Scripture for hours on end—for "as long as time permits."[6] In the early third century, Hippolytus assumed that the first duty of Christians would be to sit and listen to Scripture—"to hear the Word."[7] There was a time commitment involved in the hearing of God's word.

In light of this required commitment, how can we offer God true and acceptable worship if Scripture is not given a prominent place in our worship? Many churches today do not even encourage their people to bring Bibles to church (printed or electronic); and instead project all Scripture read in the worship service on screens for all to see. When this is the case, why would people bring their Bibles to church? Furthermore, if we do not teach people how to use their Bibles in church, how will they know how to use them at home without the passages of Scripture conveniently placed on a screen in front of them? As a result, have we lost the importance of

6. Martyr, *First and Second Apologies*, 67.
7. Hippolytus, *Treatise on the Apostolic Tradition*, 15.

the word of God in our lives? Worse yet, have we lost respect for the word? Robert Webber recalls:

> On one occasion, when I was nine years old, I happened to see my father wrapping his Bible in newspaper. "What are you doing, Dad," I asked. "This is an old Bible that I am planning to bury in the back yard," he answered. "Because this is God's Word, it is important to always treat it with reverence. I've worn this Bible out and bought a new one. It would be irreverent to throw it in the trash, so I'm burying it."
>
> My father had a point. The Bible is the record of God's living action and speech to us; therefore, it ought to be treated with the greatest reverence and respect. I have found this to be true, not only in my personal life, but also in my worship.[8]

If we believe the word of God to be of high importance in our worship, it should be seen and heard in our worship gatherings. Scripture should permeate the entire worship service. It should be held in high regard, revered, and honored. We should see it written on signposts. We should see it written in the bulletin. We should see it projected onto screens. We should hold it in our hands being encouraged from the pulpit to follow along as we hear the word of God proclaimed. But most of all, we should hide God's word in our hearts; for when we do, our hearts will be moved and our lives will be shaped as God speaks to us through his Word.

How then has the word of God been proclaimed to God's people? How has Scripture been presented? Some would argue that Scripture is found in the songs being sung in the church service. While that may be true, and is an excellent use of Scripture, the portions of Scripture found in a song are generally short passages that have a very high potential of getting lost in the music. Scripture in song is a wonderful expression of the word of God, but it is not enough. We need to read the Bible as well, because most people do not read it on their own and have little to no encouragement to do so since many church leaders are not modeling it for them.

> For most people sitting in the church on a given morning, the pastor knows that his Scripture readings and references will be the only ones to which they will be exposed during the week. Only 4 out of every 10 adults will read any portion of the Bible outside the

---

8. Webber, *Worship Is a Verb*, 73–74.

church during the week . . . Those people who do read will commit about one hour to Bible reading during the week.[9]

A church I enjoy visiting while on vacation with my family has made an effort to show how important the word of God is in their time of corporate worship. As the pastor begins his sermon, he invites the congregation to open their Bibles to the text upon which he will be preaching. He then asks those without a Bible to raise their hand if they would like an usher to give them a Bible. They are told that if they do not own a Bible, they may take that one home, as a gift from the church. This makes it clear that the word of God is a high priority for that particular church.

The church can increase the amount of Scripture reading, or proclamation, in its times of worship through the addition of various elements such as:

CALL TO WORSHIP

The call to worship occurs near the beginning of the service and is the words of invitation with which a worship service begins. Oftentimes the call to worship consists of a verse or two of Scripture.

Examples

Psalm 118:24

"This is the day that the Lord has made; let us rejoice and be glad in it."

Psalm 106:1

"Praise the Lord! Oh give thanks to the Lord, for he is good; for his steadfast love endures forever."

The call to worship may also be a longer passage of Scripture. When this is the case, it is beneficial to include the congregation in the reading. Utilizing a responsive reading as a call to worship is a powerful way to incorporate the congregation. We will see a few examples of responsive readings later in this chapter.

9. Barna, *Today's Pastors*, 48.

INVOCATION

As stated in the previous chapter, an invocation is an acknowledgement of God's presence in the place of worship.

Example

Psalm 67

> "May God be gracious to us, and bless us, and make his face to shine upon us, that your way may be known on earth, your saving power among all nations.
> Let the peoples praise you, O God; let all the peoples praise you!
> Let the nations be glad and sing for joy, for you judge the peoples with equity and guide the nations upon earth.
> Let the peoples praise you, O God; let all the peoples praise you!
> The earth has yielded its increase; God, our God, shall bless us.
> God shall bless us; let all the ends of the earth fear him!"

THE PSALMS

The reading of the Psalms is one of the most acceptable forms of Scripture reading. The Psalms are replete with exhortations for the Christ-follower to praise and worship the Lord and are used often to encourage a focusing of the mind and heart on God.

Hughes Oliphant Old offers these Psalms as fairly easy for a congregation to use and follow:[10]

---

10. Old, *Leading In Prayer*, 59.

Psalm 16	Psalm 99, 100
Psalm 18	Psalm 103
Psalm 19	Psalm 104
Psalm 24	Psalm 107 (dividing it)
Psalm 33, 34	Psalm 111, 112
Psalm 46, 47, 48	Psalm 113, 114, 115
Psalm 65	Psalm 116, 117
Psalm 66, 67	Psalm 118
Psalm 68 (omitting some verses)	Psalm 119 (dividing it)
Psalm 72	Psalm 136
Psalm 73	Psalm 138
Psalm 84	Psalm 139 (omitting some verses)
Psalm 85	Psalm 145
Psalm 86, 87	Psalm 146, 147
Psalm 96	Psalm 148
Psalm 97	Psalm 149
Psalm 98	Psalm 150

CONGREGATIONAL READING

Reading the biblical text aloud, together as a congregation, is a great way to integrate corporate reading of Scripture. The public reading of Scripture is one of the most ancient, time-honored practices of God's people that is recorded in Scripture. It is a practice that is repeatedly described and commended at crucial moments in redemptive history, from the beginning to the end. In fact, it is something that God's people are specifically commanded to do with devotion. As Paul instructed Timothy, "devote yourself to the public reading of Scripture" (1 Tim 4:13). Encouraging the congregation to join together in the reading of Scripture is powerful as they are able to hear their own voices speaking God's word in unison.

THE COMMON LECTIONARY OR
REVISED COMMON LECTIONARY

The Common Lectionary or Revised Common Lectionary may be an advantageous resource for encouraging Scripture reading in the corporate setting. The lectionary takes the church through the Bible in a three-year cycle selecting passages from the Old and New Testaments. The major principle behind the lectionary is that week by week congregations would be able to hear the voice of the various Scripture writers. The lectionary helps give the church a complete understanding of who God is by looking at the entirety of Scripture over a period of time—in this case, three years.

RESPONSIVE READING

Responsive readings are effective for presenting Scripture. There is power in hearing a group or groups respond to others through the reading of Scripture. Take for instance Psalm 136, where a leader could say, "Give thanks to the Lord, for he is good" and the congregation could respond, "His love endures forever." Each time, the one voice changes the declaration of the attributes of God for which to be thankful, while the congregation, in unison, declares, "His love endures forever." This is a powerful declaration of unity for the body of Christ to proclaim God's unfailing love.

Nearly any passage of Scripture can be turned into a responsive reading. Here is one more example with an introductory statement by the worship leader:

Example

1 Chronicles 16:23–36 (with introductory statement)

David commissioned this psalm to Asaph and his brothers on the day that the ark was brought into Jerusalem. Let's read 1 Chronicles 16:23–36 responsively:

LEADER:
Sing to the LORD, all the earth; proclaim his salvation day after day.
Declare his glory among the nations, his marvelous deeds among all peoples.
CONGREGATION:
For great is the LORD and most worthy of praise; he is to be feared above all gods.
LEADER:
For all the gods of the nations are idols, but the LORD made the heavens.
CONGREGATION:

Splendor and majesty are before him; strength and joy in his dwelling place.
LEADER:
Ascribe to the LORD, O families of nations, ascribe to the LORD glory and strength, ascribe to the LORD the glory due his name.
CONGREGATION:
Bring an offering and come before him; worship the LORD in the splendor of his holiness.
LEADER:
Tremble before him, all the earth!
CONGREGATION:
The world is firmly established; it cannot be moved.
LEADER:
Let the heavens rejoice, let the earth be glad; let them say among the nations,
CONGREGATION:
"The LORD reigns!"
LEADER:
Let the sea resound, and all that is in it; let the fields be jubilant, and everything in them!
CONGREGATION:
Then the trees of the forest will sing, they will sing for joy before the LORD, for he comes to judge the earth.
LEADER:
Give thanks to the LORD, for he is good; his love endures forever.
CONGREGATION:
Cry out, "Save us, O God our Savior; gather us and deliver us from the nations, that we may give thanks to your holy name, that we may glory in your praise."
LEADER:
Praise be to the LORD, the God of Israel, from everlasting to everlasting. Then all the people said . . .
CONGREGATION:
"Amen!" "Praise the LORD."

SCRIPTURE AND SONG

Pairing Scripture and song is a great way to incorporate more Scripture within the worship service. It also has the potential of bringing more awareness and attentiveness to what is being sung.

Bless the Lord, My Soul

By integrating short portions of Psalm 145 and Psalm 103, the simple Taizé chorus, "Bless the Lord, My Soul,"[11] is given increased depth and understanding. The congregation repeatedly sings the chorus with the reading of Scripture interspersed throughout to reinforce the main theme of the song.

Bless the Lord, my soul; and bless God's holy name
Bless the Lord, my soul; who leads me into life

"I will extol you, my God and King, and bless your name forever and ever. Every day I will bless you and praise your name forever and ever" (Ps 145:1–2).

Bless the Lord, my soul; and bless God's holy name
Bless the Lord, my soul; who leads me into life

"The Lord is gracious and merciful, slow to anger and abounding in steadfast love. The Lord is good to all, and his mercy is over all that he has made" (Ps 145:8–9).

Bless the Lord, my soul; and bless God's holy name
Bless the Lord, my soul; who leads me into life

"Bless the Lord, O my soul, and forget not all his benefits, who forgives all your iniquity, who heals all your diseases, who redeems your life from the pit, who crowns you with steadfast love and mercy, who satisfies you with good so that your youth is renewed like the eagle's" (Ps 103:2–5).

Bless the Lord, my soul; and bless God's holy name
Bless the Lord, my soul; who leads me into life

"For as high as the heavens are above the earth, so great is his steadfast love toward those who fear him; as far as the east is from the west, so far does he remove our transgressions from us. As a father shows compassion to his children, so the Lord shows compassion to those who fear him. For he knows our frame; he remembers that we are dust" (Ps 103:11–14).

Bless the Lord, my soul; and bless God's holy name
Bless the Lord, my soul; who leads me into life

---

11. "Bless the Lord, My Soul," words by Robert Batastini and The Community of Taizé; music by Jacques Berthier © 1991, 1998 Ateliers et Presses de Taizé, Taizé Community, France, GIA Publications, Inc., exclusive North American agent.

DRAMATIC PRESENTATION

A dramatic presentation based on Scripture is a wonderful way to artistically communicate the word of God. There are various ways drama can be utilized to present Scripture including tableaux, readers' theater, monologues, and group presentations, among others. The following are two such examples.

Examples

Psalm 118

The following readers' theater incorporates two narrators, a group of people, and the congregation in presenting the Scripture passage; as well as a solo singing voice and percussionist to add an artistic component.

READER 1:
Oh give thanks to the Lord, for he is good; for his steadfast love endures forever!
Let Israel say,
PRESENTATION GROUP:
"His steadfast love endures forever."
READER 2:
Let the house of Aaron say,
PRESENTATION GROUP:
"His steadfast love endures forever."
READERS 1 & 2:
Let those who fear the Lord say,
EVERYONE:
"His steadfast love endures forever."
[Drums begin on toms]
READER 1:
Out of my distress I called on the Lord; the Lord answered me and set me free.
The Lord is on my side; I will not fear. What can man do to me?
The Lord is on my side as my helper; I shall look in triumph on those who hate me.
It is better to take refuge in the Lord than to trust in man.
It is better to take refuge in the Lord than to trust in princes.
All nations surrounded me; in the name of the Lord I cut them off!

They surrounded me, surrounded me on every side; in the name of the Lord I cut them off!

They surrounded me like bees; they went out like a fire among thorns; in the name of the Lord I cut them off!

I was pushed hard, so that I was falling,

[Drums stop abruptly on the word "falling"]

READER 1:

but the Lord helped me.

[Single voice begins singing "oohs"]

READER 2:

The Lord is my strength and my song; he has become my salvation.

Glad songs of salvation are in the tents of the righteous: "The right hand of the Lord does valiantly, the right hand of the Lord exalts, the right hand of the Lord does valiantly!"

I shall not die, but I shall live, and recount the deeds of the Lord.

The Lord has disciplined me severely, but he has not given me over to death.

Open to me the gates of righteousness, that I may enter through them and give thanks to the Lord.

[Drums begin again]

READER 1:

This is the gate of the Lord; the righteous shall enter through it.

I thank you that you have answered me and have become my salvation.

The stone that the builders rejected has become the cornerstone.

READER 2:

This is the Lord's doing; it is marvelous in our eyes.

This is the day that the Lord has made; let us rejoice and be glad in it.

READERS 1 & 2:

Save us, we pray, O Lord!

READER 1:

O Lord, we pray, give us success!

Blessed is he who comes in the name of the Lord! We bless you from the house of the Lord.

READER 2:

The Lord is God, and he has made his light to shine upon us. Bind the festal sacrifice with cords, up to the horns of the altar!

You are my God, and I will give thanks to you; you are my God; I will extol you.

[Singing voice stops "oohs"]

PRESENTATION GROUP:
Oh give thanks to the Lord, for he is good; for his steadfast love endures forever!
[Drums stop]
EVERYONE:
Oh give thanks to the Lord, for he is good; for his steadfast love endures forever!

The Parable of the Good Samaritan (Luke 10:25–37)

The following is a tableau. Tableaux are an artistic form of storytelling utilizing actors posed in frozen scenes, preferably in the middle of an action. The technique is simple: A narrator reads the text in short segments and the performers move from picture to picture without speaking. For this tableau, you should utilize three narrators: Narrator, Lawyer (Voice 1), and Jesus (Voice 2); and between eight to twelve people to play the characters: Samaritan, man who was beaten, priest, Levite, innkeeper, and a group of robbers.

NARRATOR:
And behold, a lawyer stood up to put [Jesus] to the test, saying,
VOICE 1:
"Teacher, what shall I do to inherit eternal life?"
NARRATOR:
He said to him,
VOICE 2:
"What is written in the Law? How do you read it?"
NARRATOR:
And he answered,
VOICE 1:
"You shall love the Lord your God with all your heart and with all your soul and with all your strength and with all your mind, and your neighbor as yourself."
NARRATOR:
And he said to him,
VOICE 2:
"You have answered correctly; do this, and you will live."
NARRATOR:
But he, desiring to justify himself, said to Jesus,

VOICE 1:
"And who is my neighbor?"
NARRATOR:
Jesus replied,
VOICE 2:
"A man was going down from Jerusalem to Jericho, and he fell among robbers, who stripped him and beat him and departed, leaving him half dead. [*pause**] Now by chance a priest was going down that road, and when he saw him he passed by on the other side. [*pause*] So likewise a Levite, when he came to the place and saw him, passed by on the other side. [*pause*] But a Samaritan, as he journeyed, came to where he was, and when he saw him, he had compassion. [*pause*] He went to him and bound up his wounds, pouring on oil and wine. [*pause*] Then he set him on his own animal and brought him to an inn and took care of him. [*pause*] And the next day he took out two denarii and gave them to the innkeeper, saying, 'Take care of him, and whatever more you spend, I will repay you when I come back.' [*pause*] Which of these three, do you think, proved to be a neighbor to the man who fell among the robbers?"
NARRATOR:
He said,
VOICE 1:
"The one who showed him mercy."
NARRATOR:
And Jesus said to him,
VOICE 2 [*take a step toward congregation and speak these words to them*]:
"You go, and do likewise."

each pause is for a scene change to freeze frame the part of the story just told by the narrator.

Scripture needs to find a prominent place in our worship services once again because there is authority in the Scriptures and the primary place where the church hears the authority found in Scripture is during corporate worship. This practice of corporate Scripture reading can be found dating back to the Old Testament with Moses reading aloud to the people of Israel at Mount Sinai encouraging them to remember—where they came from, who they are, and the new future they had been called to live for. Following Moses's example, Scripture was read aloud by Joshua, Josiah, and Ezra,[12] just to name a few. Jesus himself read passages from Isaiah in the synagogue and

12. I encourage you to read Nehemiah 8:1–12, noting the effect it had on the people.

the newly formed churches experienced the public reading of Paul's letters. However different we may be, when we read Scripture, we join in communion with other Christians across space and time. This means that we must be careful to make sure Scripture is read properly in public, with appropriate guidelines for choosing what to read and appropriate training that those reading Scripture do so in a manner worthy of the word of the Lord.

It also means that in our public worship, in whatever tradition, we need to make sure the reading of Scripture is viewed as important within our worship services. There has been a tendency in some places to cut back the length of readings—no doubt stemming from a desire to keep services from going too long. N. T. Wright states, "Many debates within the church have been seriously hampered because there are parts of the foundation text—a verse here, a chapter there—which have been quietly omitted from the church's public life. There is simply no excuse for leaving out verses, paragraphs or chapters, from the New Testament in particular. We dare not try to tame the Bible. It is our foundation charter; we are not at liberty to play fast and loose with it."[13]

Scripture not only encourages us in our lives as we follow Christ, it also enables us to do something. We can only get to that point by allowing Scripture to permeate our lives, shaping who we are and developing us into the men and women God has called us to be. "The written law of God gave the Israelites one of the greatest gifts of grace God has conveyed to the human race. It was given as a meeting place between God and human beings in covenant relationship with him, where the sincere heart would be received, instructed, and enabled by God to walk in his ways. When those walking in personal relationship with him receive, study, and internalize his law into their heart, it quickens and restores connection and order to the flagging soul."[14] As we study God's word we are moved to a greater understanding of what it means to become more like Christ as our inner being is spiritually formed.

As Martin Luther states, "The Bible is alive, it speaks to me; it has feet, it runs after me; it has hands, it lays hold of me."[15] The word of God serves as an avenue for God to speak directly to his people. Many consider the reading of God's word as primarily for educating people or providing material for long exegetical sermons. However, Jesus says, "the words that I speak to

13. Wright, *Last Word*, 132.
14. Willard and Johnson, *Renovation of the Heart in Daily Practice*, 148.
15. Miller, "Reformer's Early Years," 2–51.

you are spirit and life" (John 6:63). God's word is an address to his people (the congregation) expressed through reading and preaching followed by a response from his people (worship).

The use of Scripture is foundational in celebrating God in authentic worship. May the church rediscover the importance of the public presentation of Scripture. May we all remember the power and authority of God's word in our worship as we allow the word of God to richly dwell within us and form us into the likeness of Jesus Christ.

CONSIDER THIS

If Scripture is not as prominent in your worship services as you believe it should be, think of ways to begin including more Scripture passages throughout the service. Let God's voice come through multiple times in multiple ways throughout the worship service. When this is done it's usually best to carefully examine the length of each passage. A larger number of brief passages may be more effective than one long passage.

Develop a Scripture Presentation Team for your church. Be creative, yet respectful, in the way Scripture is presented to, for, and with the congregation. Be sure to rehearse the presentation of Scripture just as you would songs, including a sound check in the space where the Scripture presentation will take place. Your Scripture Presentation Team should be given the same amount of focus and energy as your musical worship team.

FOR FURTHER CONSIDERATION

Barker, Jeff. *The Storytelling Church: Adventures in Reclaiming the Role of Story in Worship.* Cleveland: Parson's Porch, 2011.
Bateman, Herbert W., IV. *Authentic Worship: Hearing Scripture's Voice, Applying Its Truths.* Grand Rapids: Kregel, 2002.

5

Communion as an Act of Worship

> When he was at table with them, he took the bread and blessed and broke it
> and gave it to them. And their eyes were opened, and they recognized him.
>
> —LUKE 24:30

WHILE SERVING AT A church in Southern California, I was asked to help develop and ultimately lead a Friday morning chapel service. The chapel service would be offered every Friday and would be open to all, which we knew would mostly consist of retired folk from our congregation that were able to make it to church on a Friday morning. It was to be held in a room in the church that had been designated as a prayer chapel. The room had a beautiful stained glass design located at the front of the room that depicted the biblical story of the prodigal son.

While members of the chapel leadership and I made plans for the service, we discussed what the service would entail and which elements of worship should be included. We considered music and preaching, offering and fellowship. That's when I brought up communion. Did we want to offer communion at Friday chapel? If so, would we follow what was done in the main Sunday morning services and offer communion once per month, or did we want to do something different? I'll never forget what happened next.

A gentleman from the senior adult leadership team spoke up. He stated that he felt doing communion once per month was not enough. He couldn't explain why, but he felt as though something in his worship was lacking due to the infrequency of communion. After further discussion, others in the group agreed with his perspective.

That moment was revealing for me. I knew I felt this way, wishing we as a church would celebrate the Lord's Supper more than once per month, just as many of our brothers and sisters do in other church traditions, but here were others from my church who felt the same way. This group of worshipers shared that they felt as though something was lacking in their worship when communion was not observed. In other words, their worship was not complete without worshiping at the Table.

As a result of this revelation, it was decided that communion would be observed every week at Friday chapel. In our planning, we determined the chapel service would follow the traditional fourfold worship pattern of gathering the people for worship, hearing from the word, offering thanksgiving at the Table, and being sent out to share God's love with the world. This is a highly recognizable pattern of worship rooted in Scripture and history, particularly the first six centuries of the church. The description in Acts 2:42 of the earliest Christian worship recounts how early Christians gathered around the apostle's teaching and the breaking of bread in the context of prayer and fellowship. This passage provides evidence that from its inception, Christian worship had two primary foci: Word and Table. Adding to that the gathering of worshipers and being sent forth into the world established the fourfold worship pattern: Gathering, Word, Table/ Thanksgiving, and Sending.

Another aspect of our Friday Chapel communion time that was regularly incorporated was utilizing the four terms of the Table found in the New Testament—the Breaking of Bread (Acts 2:42), Communion (1 Cor 10:16), the Lord's Supper (1 Cor 11), and Eucharist (1 Cor 14:16; meaning "thanksgiving"). During the instructions of the Table, I would explain one of those four terms and ask the congregation to focus on that term during the receiving of the elements. This was particularly helpful in keeping communion meaningful each week as well as informative since many had never thought through the four terms. I was able to educate the congregation and encourage their worship as they gave thanks to God for his gift of salvation through Jesus Christ.

In the two and half years that I assisted in leading Friday chapel at the church, we observed communion every week. Each time, it was a special moment of worship for those in attendance.

❖ ❖ ❖

An important question to ask before we go any further is, does repetition diminish the meaning of a worship element and hinder spiritual formation from taking place? I waited to ask this question until now because this is a common inquiry when it comes to participating in communion. The former question seems to be the prevalent theme for the debate on the frequency in observing the Lord's Supper. Some have told me, "If it's done too regularly, it becomes rote and it doesn't mean as much." Yet, performing tasks ritualistically is not necessarily bad. I brush my teeth every day—multiple times throughout the day, in fact. I'm quite confident that those in whom I come into contact with are grateful for that ritual in my life. There are plenty of rituals in our lives that positively develop us into functional human beings. How much more should our spiritual development by connecting with God through communion be an important part of the regular routine of our lives?

Our time of worship at the Table will hopefully leave us changed. As we participate in communion, our hearts should burn within us as we remember that the one who was crucified, dead, buried, and rose again is now alive and within us. This leads the worshiper into the mysterious greatness of God.

This mystery of God's total self-giving love is best described in the word "communion." In communion, God, in and through Jesus, "wants, not only to teach us, instruct us, or inspire us, but to become one with us. God desires to be fully united with us so that all of God and all of us can be bound together in a lasting love."[16] We are informed by Jesus himself that just as vines are interwoven throughout the branches of a plant, those who believe (the branches) in Jesus, and abide in him (the vine), will have union with him by faith, growing spiritually and bearing fruit (John 15:1–8). When we come to the Lord's Table, we are reminded to seek to live more in the fullness of Christ, and to grow more fruitful in every good word and deed, so our joy in him and in his salvation may be full.

Correspondingly, at the Lord's Table we remember all that Christ has done for us and we give thanks for his atoning sacrifice through his death on the cross. Yet we are invited to a greater understanding that we do not find our atonement strictly through Christ's sacrifice, for in fact, Christ himself is our atonement. Through this process, we are being transformed as we gain a greater understanding of who God is and what he has done for us in Christ. We remember, as we are instructed to do (1 Cor 11:23–26),

16. Nouwen, *With Burning Hearts*, 85–86.

his suffering, death, resurrection, and the entirety of his salvation story. "What nourishes and transforms us at bread and wine is the disclosure of the whole story of God—creation, incarnation, re-creation—which takes up residence inside of us as we take and eat, take and drink. For in this symbol a reality is present—the divine action of God redeeming his world through Jesus Christ . . . We become what we eat—living witnesses to Christ who lives in us."[17] The idea of becoming what we eat is an impeccable description of spiritual formation, particularly when discussing communion. As we participate in the spiritual act of remembering Christ's death and resurrection through communion, just as bread and cup nourish our physical bodies, God offers us spiritual nutrition to the building up of spiritual health. This becomes to us a consistent gift of spiritual formation.

By now you have figured out that there are several terms associated with the Table. We have seen some of them already in this chapter. Let's consider these biblical terms: Eucharist, the Lord's Supper, Communion, and Breaking of Bread.

EUCHARIST

The English word eucharist is from the Greek *eucharistia*, meaning "thanksgiving." Both Mark (Mark 14:22–23) and the apostle Paul (1 Cor 11:24) used the term. Eucharist does not prompt a somber manner of giving thanks, but a thanksgiving filled with joy and celebration, which is certainly appropriate as the emphasis of eucharist is on the resurrection. When we come to the Table, we not only ponder the death of our Savior on the cross, but also the power of God that raised Jesus from the dead. Therefore, approaching the Table eucharistically—with joyful thanksgiving and celebration—is an appropriate act of worship for the church.

THE LORD'S SUPPER

The Lord's Supper may be the most common term used by Protestants for the Table, finding its biblical connection to the Last Supper where Jesus joined with his disciples in an upper room for the Passover meal the evening before his crucifixion. While at this memorial meal, Jesus instituted a new covenant and commanded his followers to eat the bread and drink the

---

17. Webber, *Ancient-Future Worship*, 146.

wine in remembrance of his body and blood offered as a sacrifice for the world. Later, the apostle Paul refers to this instance as the Lord's Supper, *kuriakos deipnon* (1 Cor 11:20).

The emphasis of the Lord's Supper is in remembering the sacrifice of Jesus on the cross. Participating at the Table in this way has a memorial view and will oftentimes be accompanied by a solemn or somber atmosphere, reminiscent of a funeral or memorial service.

COMMUNION

The English word communion is derived from the Greek word *koinonia*, which is translated as "participation," "sharing," or "fellowship." The essential meaning of *koinonia* embraces concepts conveyed in the term community. It is a Christian fellowship or communion, with God or, more commonly, with other Christians. Many of the elements of worship that we participate in within a worship service can be done on our own—singing, praying, reading of God's word—but communion is one that must be done in community. Both Paul and Luke use *koinonia* to emphasize the communal nature of the Table. Luke uses it in reference to the actions of the gathered church, where he includes the breaking of bread (Acts 2:42). Paul uses the same word in addressing the Corinthians regarding the importance of participating together in the bread and cup (1 Cor 10:16–17). Communion is an act of worship that is done together with other followers of Christ.

BREAKING OF BREAD

We are told in the book of Acts that the earliest Christian community devoted themselves to the breaking of bread (Acts 2:42). This expression is a way of describing a shared meal. If a person eats alone, he does not need to break the bread because there is nobody to share it with. However, if you are eating with others, the loaf of bread must be broken into pieces so everyone is included. Historians believe the breaking of bread referred to a regular meal, most likely daily, which included the celebration of bread and cup. The devotion of followers of Christ to this practice is evidenced by Acts 2:46–47a: "And day by day, attending the temple together and breaking bread in their homes, they received their food with glad and generous hearts, praising God and having favor with all the people." We see that in early Christian times, the breaking of bread was celebrated as part of an ordinary meal for which the followers of Jesus were gathered in his name in a private home. The remembrance of Jesus's death and resurrection would be included in the midst of, or near the end of, the shared meal. Ultimately, the breaking of bread refers to the fact that the church is a communal group, sharing with one another in the love of Jesus.

There is a story in Scripture that tells us of a disciple named Cleopas and his friend (Luke 24:13–35). They were walking on a road, traveling from Jerusalem, and Jesus joined them. The interesting part of the story is that they did not recognize Jesus. After walking and talking with Jesus for a while, they arrived near their home and invited Jesus to stay for a meal. It was at this meal that the miraculous occurs.

> When he was at table with them, he took the bread and blessed and broke it and gave it to them. And their eyes were opened, and they recognized him. And he vanished from their sight. They said to each other, "Did not our hearts burn within us while he talked to us on the road, while he opened to us the Scriptures?" (Luke 24:30–32)

Cleopas and his friend walked with Jesus, talked with Jesus, even ate dinner with Jesus, but did not recognize him. It wasn't until the "breaking of bread" (one of the terms regularly used throughout Scripture for communion) that their eyes were opened and they recognized (and knew—see Luke 24:35) Jesus. Constance Cherry, reflecting upon this biblical account, states,

> Much dialogue took place between Jesus and the disciples traveling the road together from Jerusalem to Emmaus on the day of the resurrection. The episodes of conversation are readily seen. . . . Yet when you look at the entire story, you see that Jesus succeeded in weaving the dialogue into something much more significant than mere conversation. There was a transformation in the disciples that took place over time as a result of the whole conversation. Their encounter with Jesus was not a journey because they were traveling the same road together. Rather, their encounter was a journey because they progressed spiritually—from their place of origin (grief and confusion), through necessary terrain (explanation of the Scriptures), and finally, to their destination (recognizing the risen Lord).[18]

---

18. Cherry, *Worship Architect*, 15–16.

Likewise, at the Table of the Lord, our eyes are opened to the wonder of Jesus and our hearts burn with the power of the Holy Spirit. When we come to the Table, we don't simply remember a past event, but allow the past remembrance to become a present experience. The Greek word for remembrance used at the Table ("Do this in remembrance of me"), is *anamnesis*, as we saw in chapter 1. A number of years ago, as I was dropping my youngest son off at preschool, I stepped out of the car and the smell of coffee cake from the middle school next door wafted my direction. The smell of the coffee cake immediately ushered me back to my middle school days. I stood there as a grown man, a husband, and a father, yet everything within me felt as though I were in middle school again. All because of a smell that forced a past remembrance into a present experience. This is the meaning of *anamnesis*. Too often we remember past events without allowing them to affect our worship today. However, *anamnesis* at the Table of the Lord allows us to relive for ourselves the saving events of Christ.

Throughout Scripture we encounter multiple themes that encourage us in experiencing the God of the Table. Although there are more, I'd like to focus on three themes here: Passover, Covenant, and the Wedding Feast/Banquet.

PASSOVER

In the upper room, Jesus took a familiar, annual meal and gave it new meaning connecting his sacrificial death with the deliverance of the Israelites out of slavery in Egypt. Just as the blood of the lambs was shed and covered the doorposts of the Israelites homes, sparing them from death, so Jesus's blood now covers us, sparing us from death. Jesus has become the Passover Lamb, sacrificed for our deliverance.

The Passover was a special meal. God knows that we humans are a forgetful people so he instructed his covenant people to remember and celebrate the event every year (Exod 12:14–20). In a similar way Jesus instructed his disciples to commemorate him when they received the bread and the cup.

COVENANT

When Jesus referred to the cup of the new covenant in his blood, the disciples most likely recalled the event at Mount Sinai when God ratified his covenant with Israel by having Moses sprinkle blood on the people, following the reading of the Book of the Covenant (Exod 24:8–9). They probably also remembered that this dramatic event was followed by a meal, as Moses, Aaron, Nadab, Abihu, and seventy of the elders went up on the mountain. "But God did not raise his hand against these leaders of the Israelites; they saw God, and they ate and drank" (Exod 24:11).

The leaders of Israel saw God, and they ate and drank in his presence as a way to affirm this agreement with God. But over the next 1,400 years, people broke God's covenant through their disobedience. This is why God the Father sent Jesus Christ his Son into the world to make a new Covenant (Jer 31:31–34). It's a new agreement between God and people offering widespread salvation to any who will trust in Jesus. In order to ratify this new covenant, Jesus invited his twelve disciples to a meal. Furthermore, he invites all who believe in him to participate in the meal—through the Table of the Lord as we gather for corporate worship and by means of the marriage supper of the Lamb when we gather together in heaven.

WEDDING BANQUET

As the early church celebrated the Lord's Supper, it was with the expectation of Jesus's imminent return and the consummation of creation (1 Cor 11:26). Moreover, John's eschatological vision includes the long-awaited union of Christ and his bride, the church. "Let us rejoice and exult and give him the glory, for the marriage of the Lamb has come, and his Bride has made herself ready" (Rev 19:7). Those who have accepted Christ, and thus have become heirs of Christ, are invited to a grand feast celebrating this union. "Blessed are those who are invited to the marriage supper of the Lamb" (Rev 19:9). This resonates with the promise of Jesus, "People will come from east and west, and from north and south, and recline at table in the kingdom of God" (Luke 13:29).

Henri Nouwen sums up this *prolepsis*, or anticipation, in this way:

> Communion with Jesus means becoming like him. With him we are nailed on the cross, with him we are laid in the tomb, with him we are raised up to accompany lost travelers on their journey. Communion, becoming Christ, leads us to a new realm of being. It ushers us into the Kingdom.[19]

19. Nouwen, *With Burning Hearts*, 94.

The following is a charming story written in a blog post by Tom Lawson:[20]

"And it was right then," the old man continued, "that I saw magic."

You could feel the room grow quiet. Even people who knew what was coming couldn't wait to hear it again.

"I saw it. Real honest-to-God magic. Not the sleight-of-hand we've all seen at parties. I'm talking about actual magic. No fooling. Something that's just downright impossible. But, I saw it. Saw it with my own two eyes."

You could have heard a pin drop. Everyone held their breath, waiting to hear the rest of the story.

"The man was sitting right across from me. No further than I am from you." He pointed to one of the teenagers sitting on the floor.

"Well, you've got to know that real magic doesn't come with light or smoke or a big bang. You are just looking right at something that's as ordinary as can be and then, you no more than blink, and it's already happened. It takes a second or two for your brain to catch up to what your eyes just saw."

He knew he was stretching the story out a little too far. He could feel the growing impatience as everyone leaned almost imperceptibly forward. It was time for the big climax.

"And so, the guy just reached down, picked up the bread, said the words, and then . . . magic. That's when I looked up and saw him. Plain as day. Sitting right there. For a second, I was too surprised to move or say anything."

"And then, just like that," the old man snapped his fingers, "He disappeared." "Where'd he go?" one of the girls in the back blurted out before she could stop herself. "Go?" the old man smiled. "Did I say *go*? He didn't *go* anywhere. I just said he disappeared." "But . . . So you're saying he was still there?" "He was still there. I was looking right at him." "But you said he disappeared." There were murmurs and nods. It didn't make any sense.

Then one of the mothers who'd been listening said out loud the thought that came to her. "It was the bread! You were looking at the bread." The old man smiled. It was usually a woman who figured it out first. "Yes, it was the bread. I could see him. See him right there in front of me. He was hiding in plain sight in that broken loaf of bread on the table."

20. Lawson, "Magic Story," 2012.

"The words," someone pleaded. "Tell us the words he said. Just before the magic." "He had lifted up the bread, broke it, and then said, 'This is my body.' Those were the words."

The old man's Latin wasn't that great. But, it was good enough to tell a story he'd told hundreds of times. The story about the man and the bread and the words. *Hoc est corpus meum. This is my body.* He knew his accent probably made *hoc est corpus* sound more like *hocus pocus*. But that's how it happened. He'd been witness to magic.

The Only Son. Eternally begotten. True God of true God. And, now, he had told them all the story of how this very Jesus was made known to him in the breaking of bread. The story was done. Cleopas knew it was all about to happen again. It was time for Communion.

(And, by the way, the expression *hocus-pocus* as a synonym for magic did evolve from "this is my body" or "the body of Christ" [*hoc est corpus Christi*] as it was used in the Medieval Latin mass in England).

We must come to the Table with a sense of anticipation, believing that the Lord will meet us there in a unique way. At the Table we are nourished and transformed as we rehearse the story of God. For in communion we discover the mystery of God and the redemption of the world through Jesus Christ. We remember all God has done culminating in Christ's sacrifice and we anticipate the future day when we will participate in a great banquet feast with Christ. We are spiritually changed as we engage in the partaking of bread and cup.

CONSIDER THIS

The regular observance of communion can become commonplace for some in your congregation. Consider incorporating creative ideas to help your congregation experience communion in a fresh way. Here are three options:

1. Involve All Five Senses

   Smell—incense or a bread machine baking in the background
   Sight—a decorative banner or image on screen
   Hearing—recreate the sound of the hammer on nails
   Touch—the bread
   Taste—the cup

2. Clean Hands and Pure Heart

Emphasize "clean hands and pure heart" (Ps 51). Invite the congregation to rinse their hands in a basin before approaching the Lord's Table.

3. One Loaf, One Body

If you generally use small crackers and individual cups served to the congregation in rows, try changing the format by inviting the congregation to come forward to the table while using a whole loaf and one cup, requiring people to tear off their own piece of bread and dip or drink from a common cup.

FOR FURTHER CONSIDERATION

Galbreath, Paul. *Leading from the Table*. Herndon: Alban Institute, 2008.

Nouwen, Henri. *With Burning Hearts: A Meditation on the Eucharistic Life*. Maryknoll: Orbis, 1994.

Stookey, Laurence H. *Eucharist: Christ's Feast with the Church*. Nashville: Abingdon, 1993.

Wright, N. T. *The Meal Jesus Gave Us: Understanding Holy Communion*. Louisville: Westminster John Knox, 1999.

6

Sermon as an Act of Worship

All Scripture is breathed out by God and profitable for teaching, for reproof, for correction, and for training in righteousness, that the man of God may be complete, equipped for every good work.

—2 TIMOTHY 3:16–17

Throughout my ministry, I have served as a guest worship leader and worship consultant in various churches. If ever I had a Sunday off from official ministry work, my family would attend a local church, Grace Church, in our hometown. We attended Grace, not only because the worship service as a whole was solid in quality, but because the sermons were theologically deep, practical in application, and delivered by the empowerment of the Holy Spirit. God has used the preaching elders at Grace to challenge their congregation to a deeper relationship with God. All those who share the pulpit take 2 Timothy 3:16–17 to heart—"All Scripture is breathed out by God and profitable for teaching, for reproof, for correction, and for training in righteousness, that the man of God may be complete, equipped for every good work." There is a strong desire to preach the word with clarity, conviction, and boldness, anointed of the Holy Spirit.

Preaching at Grace joins every other element in the worship service in offering worship to God. Scripture permeates the entire worship service— songs, readings, prayers, etc.—and the sermon is one offering of worship among the many offered throughout the service.

Unfortunately, many churches today are not focused on solid biblical preaching. One church I served had the expectation that the worship service would last no longer than one hour. That was fine except that the senior pastor was determined to preach a forty-minute sermon; or, 67 percent of the worship service was to be devoted to the congregation seated, listening to the sermon. To further complicate the issue, the sermon, although based on Scripture, was primarily filled with inspirational, motivational speech, rather than Scripture that challenged the congregation toward being fully committed followers of Christ. As the worship leader, I took it upon myself to focus on spiritual formation through the other elements of worship within the service.

Author Warren Wiersbe shares this thoughtful prayer in regard to the preaching of a sermon:

> Father,
>
> I know You have forgiven me for my sins. But can You ever forgive me for my sermons?
>
> Forgive me for being clever, for presenting Your truth in neat human packages that robbed You of glory. Forgive me for preaching to impress rather than to express. Forgive me for predictable preaching that lacked surprises and heavenly interruptions. Help me to so open the word that hearts will burn and people will say, "We have seen the Lord!" May each message be fresh from the altar, fragrant with heavenly incense and ignited by divine fire. Remind me, O Lord, of the awesomeness of preaching. Convict me when I find it easy to manufacture outlines and feed my people on substitutes. Apart from You, Lord, I can do nothing. With You, I can do all things. I don't want to be a preacher only. Please, make me Your messenger. Whatever it is that I must burn up—here are the ashes. Reveal Yourself to me, and help me to reveal You to others as I proclaim Your word.
>
> In Jesus's Name, Amen.

❖ ❖ ❖

The ministry of proclaiming the word of God through the preaching of a sermon must be an act of worship. If the sermon is not an act of worship, then the church may end up worshiping the preacher rather than worshiping God. Reformer Martin Luther stated, "When I declare the Word of God, I offer sacrifice, when thou hearest the Word of God with all thy heart, thou dost offer sacrifice."

Additionally, R. J. Coates and J. I. Packer share, "Preaching, if not sacramental, is profane. By this we mean that a true sermon is an act of God, and not a mere performance by man. In real preaching the speaker is the servant of the Word and God speaks and works by the Word through his servant's lips."[1]

As we have seen in the previous chapter, the book of Acts tells of the early church, "they devoted themselves to the apostles' teaching and the fellowship, to the breaking of bread and the prayers" (Acts 2:42). The Greek for the English word "teaching" found in this passage is *kerygma*. That term *kerygma* means to proclaim and it has to do with the preaching, or proclaiming, of the message of Jesus Christ. The Greek word *kerygma* is translated "preach" six times in Acts. Two additional passages to utilize the Greek word *kerygma* (underlined translation) are:

> And he said to them, "Go into all the world and *proclaim* the gospel to the whole creation." (Mark 16:15)

> Jews demand signs and Greeks seek wisdom, but we *preach* Christ crucified. (1 Cor 1:22–23)

Kerygma calls people to faith, to discipleship, to spiritual formation. It calls people to conversion, convicting, repentance, and the transformation of lives.

Many churches today do not view the sermon as an act of worship. A great number of the sermons proclaimed in churches today have become overly academic. We have turned our sanctuaries into lecture halls, complete with overhead projectors and lecture notes. Preachers feel as though they have to explain and outline everything. This turns the sermon into an intellectual event rather than a worship experience. I agree with Warren Wiersbe when he states that "the most important thing about a sermon should be what God writes on our hearts as we see him in the Word, not what we write in our notebooks!"[2]

We have a tendency to overanalyze and explain everything, leaving out the mystery of God in the process. True worship, however, invites mystery and wonder because God is filled with mystery and wonder. The apostle Paul knew better than to think he had figured out everything there was to know about God. At the conclusion of his letter to the Romans, after focusing on the sovereignty of God, he is moved to worshiping in awe and wonder:

1. Packer, *Beyond the Battle for the Bible*, 84.
2. Wiersbe, *Real Worship*, 123.

> Oh, the depths of the riches and wisdom and knowledge of God!
> How unsearchable are his judgments and how inscrutable his
> ways! (Rom 11:33)

Even Paul, author of much of the New Testament, didn't feel compelled to explain everything. He left some things to the realm of mystery.

If not academic, we often turn our sermons into pep rally cheers. I have known preachers who consider themselves "inspirational preachers." Unfortunately, this often turns the preacher into nothing more than a cheerleader leading cheers on the sidelines instead of taking on the challenge of getting in the game. This is the example the congregation sees and ultimately mimics. This style of inspirational preaching usually does not effectively challenge the congregation to deep spiritual living. The inspirational preacher is generally more concerned with inspiring the people that he neglects other important roles of the preacher; to reprove, rebuke, and exhort (2 Tim 4:1–3). The Scripture passage continues with Timothy saying that the people, when spiritually neglected, will search out teachers to suit their own passions. This sounds to me like a preacher that is more of a pep rally cheerleader than a teacher of sound doctrine.

Scripture as the foundation of the sermon provides the preacher with authority that can only be found in the word of God. The preacher has the power to be direct and confident while proclaiming, "thus says the Lord." Inspirational preaching on the other hand has the potential of leaving the congregation with the opinion of being manipulated and/or coerced into feeling or believing a certain way. Gary Furr and Milburn Price state,

> The "scripting" of preaching can, like a bad play, be predictable
> and dull. Even worse, it can be manipulative. A play is said to be
> "preachy" when it uses the medium of drama to coerce a certain
> (and unvarying) response. Good preaching is direct, understand-
> able, and dynamic, but it also has a certain quality of open-ended-
> ness. It is evocative—it stirs and 'opens up' without substituting for
> the work of the Spirit.[3]

In his sermon entitled "The Crisis Of This World" delivered on October 6, 1889, at the Metropolitan Tabernacle in London, preacher Charles Spurgeon challenged his congregation, and us, with these words:

> I do believe that we slander Christ when we think that we are to
> draw the people by something else but the preaching of Christ

---

3. Furr and Price, *Dialogue of Worship*, 11.

crucified . . . Preach Christ and men will be drawn to him, for so the text says, "I, if I am lifted up from the earth, will draw all men unto Me." They are held back by Satan, but the cross will draw them. They are held back by despair, but the cross will attract them. They are held back by lack of desire, but the cross will breed desire. They are held back by love of sin, but the cross will make them hate the sin that crucified the Savior. "I will draw them. All sorts of men I will draw unto myself," says the crucified Christ. Thus he supplies our great need.

Our sermons must not be turned into inspirational cheers, motivational speeches, or political agendas. Our sermons must be filled with the word of God. They must be gospel driven. For it is only by the power of God and his words that lives can be transformed.

There are a variety of ways to approach the delivery of a sermon. Preachers generally gravitate toward one type of sermon over another. These include Expository, Topical, Textual, Bible Story, and Narrative sermons.

The *Expository Sermon*, as the name implies, is delivered by way of Bible exposition. This way of preaching details the meaning of a particular text or passage of Scripture. It explains what the Bible means by what it says. Exegesis is technical and grammatical exposition, a careful drawing out of the exact meaning of a passage in its original context.

There are several advantages to the expository sermon. For one, a preacher can create a sermon series based on one single context, particularly a book of the Bible. It seems as though the apostles used this manner of preaching. Also, expository preaching promotes solid biblical foundation. It protects the preacher of being accused of preaching to individuals and using the pulpit for personal attacks or retaliation especially when conflict inside the church arises. Finally, expository preaching promotes solid exegesis because the message is simply within the given passage of Scripture.

The *Topical Sermon* focuses mainly on a particular topic, or a topic within the scriptural text. The points of the sermon do not necessarily come from one single text, but are usually invented by the preacher guided by the assorted possibilities of the subject in accordance with the Bible and the preacher's knowledge concerning the topic.

The advantages for this kind of sermon are that it allows the preacher to have freedom in composition and full treatment of any subject, and it helps the preacher to be more creative, opening the door for linguistic eloquence. There are some dangers, however, in using this type of sermon often. The content of the sermon is basically at the mercy of the preacher

SERMON AS AN ACT OF WORSHIP

instead of what Scripture is saying. More often it is too general in scope while the portion being presented is only a small part of the main idea. There are numerous possibilities that the preacher can abuse the exegetical rules in order to fit it in his sermon, especially text passages from different points with different settings and context. There is a tendency for the topical sermon to be too secular in form as well as a tendency for the preacher to present his own personal views and prejudices rather than what the Bible truly states. Topical sermons are good for preachers who do not preach frequently, but are not too helpful for regular preachers since it is more difficult to think of supplementary topics rather than allowing the word of God to speak to us.

The main difference between the topical sermon and the *Textual Sermon* is that in textual sermons, topics do not just come out of what the preacher is thinking but of what the passage is stating. The points, though added or invented by the preacher, are clearly a part of the Scripture passage. In addition, among the three kinds of sermons looked at thus far—expository, topical, and textual—I would say that the textual sermon is half expository and half topical.

The textual sermon also possesses some advantages since it is more scriptural in design compared to the topical sermon. The points of a textual sermon are predictable since they can be found in the text. It also permits a variety of construction and selection of the preacher. The hearers of the textual sermon will not be left hanging with unfocused thoughts since all the divisions and points can be found in the text. This type of sermon is most likely to be remembered because there will be a "memory connection" between the passage and the sermon at the back of the mind of the hearers.

Some consider the *Bible-Story Sermon* and the *Narrative Sermon* to be similar, if not the same. However, for the purpose of clearly delineating between the fictional/experiential stories of the narrative sermon with the Bible-story sermon, I will refer to experiential and fictional stories later when I discuss narrative sermons. Bible-story sermons are about telling the stories of the Bible then delivering an application found from within the Bible story. It is important to look for spiritual truths that lie within the Bible story that can be communicated to the congregation in order to help form them into the likeness of Jesus Christ. After seeing the spiritual truths within the story, the preacher will attempt to summarize these truths in a sermon outline.

Some of the advantages of Bible-story sermons are that they are purely Bible-based, which I believe to be the strongest advantage. Preaching this type of sermon is more creative than that of any traditional way of preaching. It is important to communicate that Bible stories are not only for kids but for all ages. Bible-story preaching enhances our knowledge about the truths in Bible stories. If you are a regular preacher, it is easy to plan ahead of time what Bible stories you are going to preach through since the Bible is composed of approximately 70–80 percent story form content. The main disadvantage with Bible-story preaching is that the preacher who does not have a talent in story telling will find it more difficult to use.

The Narrative sermon is similar to the Bible-story sermon because it also deals with stories. The big difference, however, lies with the story itself. In narrative preaching, the preacher uses experience and fictional stories and then quotes passages from the Bible to make a point, while Bible-story preaching uses Bible stories to deliver God's word.

Here's a simple process to get a picture of the narrative sermon: The preacher tells a fictional or an experiential story. Most of them are quite long, oftentimes enough to consume ten to fifteen minutes of the sermon to tell it. After telling the story, the preacher will quote a passage which is very much related to the story and then present concise points. Making an excellent conclusion is crucial since this will tell the people if the story is really worth noting. The main issue raised against narrative preaching, and which is worth evaluating, is the issue of its source of message, because narrative preaching is not purely Bible based.

Scripture is the source of all truth and is the vehicle through which the Holy Spirit does his refining, sharpening work to make us more like Christ. No matter what type of sermon is chosen as the delivery system, the word of God must be the driving force. It is through the truth of God's word that the Holy Spirit can form our inner beings into imitators of Jesus Christ.

In conclusion, consider these words from Frank Cairns, spoken during his Warnack Lectures in 1934:

> Gentlemen, if you are ever to serve God by your preaching, you have got to make up your mind as to whether it had or has not the right to be regarded as an essential part of the worship of God; you must have a clear idea as to whether your preaching is for you an act of worship—an offering to God which you can make with a clear conscience, and a wholehearted devotion, and humble faith, or whether it is something which—be it either cheap or tawdry, or manifesting both erudition and literary skill—could not be

regarded as possessing the authority of the Word of God or any Divine Sanction whatsoever, and which might as well be tied in a napkin and buried in the earth for all the value it has for the purpose of bringing the human soul face-to-face with God.[4]

The purpose of the word of God is to reveal the God of the word. In Scripture, the people who saw God were never quite the same again. Their lives were transformed. So it should be every worship service in which the word is proclaimed.

CONSIDER THIS

As mentioned in the introduction, there have been Christian leaders recently that have renounced their faith. This illustrates the importance of preaching the gospel with clarity and conviction.

Pastor, before preaching your sermon, ask yourself whether Jesus is clearly seen in every aspect of the sermon. Seeing Jesus in the Bible, both Old and New Testaments, is reading the Bible the way it is intended; preaching gospel driven sermons is preaching the Bible the way it is intended—with Christ as the primary subject.

Congregation, as you hear the sermon being preached, look for Christ in every aspect of the sermon. Unless you are a brand-new believer, you do not need the preacher to spoon-feed you. Your relationship with God allows you to feed yourself from the table set by the preacher and the Holy Spirit.

FOR FURTHER CONSIDERATION

Chapell, Bryan. *Christ-Centered Sermons: Models of Redemptive Preaching*. Grand Rapids: Baker Academic, 2013.

4. Cairns, *Prophet of the Heart*, 56–57.

7

Stillness as an Act of Worship

> Be still, and know that I am God. I will be exalted among the nations, I will be exalted in the earth!
>
> —Psalm 46:10

Have you ever known someone who likes to talk? Not necessarily because they like to hear themselves speak (we know those types of people as well), but because they genuinely have a lot to say. I have one of those in my family . . . my youngest son.

I can recall one time when my family was sitting in church together and the pastor asked a similar question to the one I asked above: Do you know someone who is a talker? My oldest son leaned over to me and pointed in the direction of his brother. The fact that my youngest son is a talker is common knowledge in our family. I don't think he likes to talk . . . he loves to talk.

He's been a talker for as long as I can remember. Take, for instance, the time when he was six years old. You may not know it, but six-year-olds have a lot to say. He loved to tell us about his day at school and he would tell us about Bible stories he learned at church. He would tell us about the books his school teacher read to the class and about the songs he liked to sing. About video games and his favorite TV shows. His favorite things to eat and how, where, when, and why he liked to eat them. It really didn't matter what it was, he would tell you about it. Oftentimes, he would simply narrate what he was doing as he was doing it, not talking to anyone in particular. He was/is a talker.

His elementary school is a mile from our home. One morning, as we were walking to school, my son began to talk. I can't remember what it was about, but it was extremely interesting to him and it seems as though he didn't take a breath for ten minutes. He talked from the doorstep of our home until we reached the gate of his school. I'm not sure he was even aware he was talking.

Most of the time, it made me laugh. Other times it drove me crazy. Sometimes, his mother and I would look at him and say, "Okay, it's time to stop talking now and just be quiet." He would look at us and say, "I'm not talking." He wasn't being deceptive. I believe he truly didn't realize he was talking.

I imagine the same happens in our times of worship. We come before God and we talk, talk, talk . . . and God says, "Okay, it's time to stop talking now and just be quiet. Just sit back, quiet yourself, receive from me, and know that I am God." And we respond, "I'm not talking."

❖ ❖ ❖

Since worship is our response to God as he has revealed himself, much of our worship is filled with words and actions that require of us to speak, sing, and do. Yet there is power in the simple response of being still before the Lord. When God spoke to Elijah on Mount Horeb, he could have done so in the wind, an earthquake, or through fire. But God chose instead to speak with a "still small voice" (1 Kgs 19:12). Likewise, the Psalmist reminds us to "be still, and know" that he is God (Ps 46:10). The more we focus on God, the more we will experience reprieve from those things in our lives that attempt to drown out the voice of God. It's time for us to quiet our hearts and listen for him as we meditate on his word. For in times of stillness, we not only have the opportunity to hear from God but to also respond.

MEDITATION

Depending on your church tradition and background, the word meditation will either stir-up thoughts of affirmation or yield trepidation within your mind. The New Illustrated Bible Dictionary states that meditation today is a "lost art for many Christians." Some of our popular Bible translations even substitute other words when they translate "meditate" or "meditation" in the Scriptures. Today the church has virtually surrendered meditation to the New Age Movement and to Eastern religions. However, we should not be willing to surrender this biblical practice. The Bible makes it clear that meditation belongs to the children of God. People have a deep spiritual need to meditate, whether they realize it or not, and it is certainly for this reason that some people with Christian backgrounds have been drawn into cults.

The Bible tells us it is important to think about God's word. Our thoughts determine our behavior and so what we think about is critically important. That is why God wants us to think about his word, or meditate on it.

I would like for us to consider meditation in the simplest and most innocent of ways for the purpose of this chapter. Discussing meditation here is not about magic or Eastern mysticism. That is the world's version of meditation. The word meditation simply means to think deeply or carefully about. It is the slow and constant turning over of a thought or idea. If you know how to worry, you already know how to meditate. How much more advantageous to meditate on Scripture than the worries that come our way?

Some have likened meditation to a cow chewing on its cud. The cow savors the grass in its mouth before filling its stomach. Then it sits down in the meadow and quietly regurgitates the grass, reworking it in its mouth before swallowing it. It may not sound appealing, but the process transforms the grass into rich, creamy milk. In the same way the word of God is meant to become pure spiritual milk for us (1 Pet 2:2). When we meditate on God's word we take it from our mind down into our heart for prayer. Meditating on God's word encourages us as worshipers to "taste and see that the Lord is good" (Ps 34:8). Our mind is renewed and our whole being is transformed (Rom 12:1–2). We're drawn into loving God, growing to trust in his love, and sharing his love with others.

It is recorded in the Bible that many of the great men of God meditated. Isaac went out into the field to meditate (Gen 24:63). The Psalmist meditated in the Law of God (Ps 1:2) and did so even in the night (Ps 63:6). He meditated on God's precepts and ways (Ps 119:15), in his statutes (Ps 119:23), and on the mighty works of God (Ps 143:5).

The Psalmist also prayed that the meditation of his heart would be sweet (Ps 104:34) and acceptable to God (Ps 19:14). Consequently we can see in Scripture that the Psalmist used meditation as a means of approaching God. His meditation then led him to greater understanding (Ps 49:3).

Even Joshua, the great leader of the Israelite tribes, spoke of the values of meditation. In Joshua 1:8 he instructs: "This Book of the Law shall not depart from your mouth, but you shall meditate on it day and night, so that you may be careful to do according to all that is written in it. For then you will make your way prosperous, and then you will have good success." A similar thought is expressed in the New Testament as Paul advises young Timothy to "Meditate on these things; give yourself entirely to them, that your progress may be evident to all" (1 Tim 4:15, NKJV).[1]

Providing an opportunity for the congregation to methodically focus on God in a worship service concentrates their attention and opens the door to a transformed mind through the work of the Holy Spirit. There are various ways in which to incorporate meditation in a Christian worship service. One way is to provide the congregation with a short phrase such as "God is merciful." Encourage the congregation to consider each word in the phrase and what each emphasis informs us about God. Ask them to think over the phrase in their mind emphasizing each word in turn: *God* is merciful. God *is* merciful. God is *merciful.*

In addition, Scripture itself is vital when it comes to meditation. Church leaders must be diligent to make sure the congregation is focused and thinking upon God and not some other idea or thought. Therefore another way to incorporate meditation in a Christian worship service is to project Scripture on the screen or print it in the bulletin, and give time for people to quietly dwell upon the word of God. Perhaps incorporate some form of art to add a creative expression resulting in greater potential of people engaging with the word of God.

Since it appears that meditation has nearly been stolen away from the church, we would do well to recover it. For I believe when we do, we will find that our lives and our worship will become much richer.

SILENCE

Silence has long been an important aspect of personal and corporate worship. It is a time to quiet the soul in order to become receptive to God's revelation. Most often, silence in worship is misunderstood, oftentimes being confused with meditation. Silence, however, is not a time for prayer, the lifting up of a supplication before the Lord, or for focusing one's attention on a particular Scripture passage. Instead, silence in worship is a time to be quiet and let God do what he wills to do. It may be a time of surrendering our thoughts, releasing our agenda, and allowing God to speak in the silence.

In *Space for God*, Don Postema quotes Emily from the Thorton Wilder play *Our Town*: "Do any human beings ever realize life while they live it—every, every minute?"[2] Our lives are so busy that we rarely stop to realize that we are alive. Silence, however, helps usher us back into the appropriate rhythms of life—and worship—leading to an openness of God's touch on our lives. "Appropriate moments of silence contribute to the rhythm of revelation and response in worship by providing "waiting space" for the revelatory work of God's Spirit."[3]

Moreover, silence is an indispensable discipline in spiritual formation. Throughout the history of the church, Christians have tried to practice the discipline of silence as a form of spiritual renewal and self-control. There is a story told in *The Sayings of the Desert Fathers* that goes: One day Archbishop Theophilus came to the desert to visit Abba Pambo. But Abba Pambo did not speak to him. When the brethren finally said to Pambo, "Father, say something to the archbishop, so that he may be edified," he replied: "If he is not edified by my silence, he will not be edified by my speech."[4]

We struggle with silence because of the world in which we live. We live in a talkative world with words inundating our lives. Wherever we go we are surrounded by words: Radio, television, streaming music, billboard signs, yard signs, electronic signs, bumper stickers, sales advertisements, and more words upon words upon words. It is difficult to escape the chattiness of our world today. Furthermore, with the constant emersion of words in our world, it has become difficult to respect and trust some of the words we hear. Have you ever heard someone say, "Those are just words"? One thing I lament about our society today is the devaluing of words. Words used to mean something. There is an old saying, "My word is my bond." Believe it or not, there was a time when you did not need a written contract with an overabundance of pages to buy or sell an item to one another. A word and a handshake was all it took. Because of the overuse of words today, oftentimes words have become powerless. Henri Nouwen expresses this in the following way:

> the main function of the word, which is communication, is no longer realized. The word no longer communicates, no longer fosters communication, no longer creates community, and therefore no

---

2. Postema, *Space for God*, 16.

3. Furr and Price, *Dialogue of Worship*, 12.

4. Ward, *Sayings of the Desert Fathers*, 69.

longer gives life. The word no longer offers trustworthy ground on which people can meet each other and build society.[5]

Nouwen continues by observing modern-day theological education compared to theological training of the past. In many of our seminaries today, the act of being in God's presence and learning to usher others into his presence gets drowned out by the complex network of discussions, debates, and arguments about God and his word. This is in comparison to the time when theological training occurred in the monastery. In a monastery, words are born out of silence, which leads to deeper silence. "Although monasteries are no longer the most common places of theological education, silence remains as indispensable today as it was in the past. The Word of God is born out of the eternal silence of God, and it is to this Word out of silence that we want to be witnesses."[6]

Musicians understand the importance of silence, or in musical terms, the rest. Music is made up of notes and rests. Any good musician understands that rests are just as important, if not more so, than the notes. For it is in the rests that the music takes shape and finds its meaning. The Taoist philosopher Chuang Tzu expresses the same sentiment when it comes to words:

> The purpose of a fish trap is to catch fish and when the fish are caught, the trap is forgotten. The purpose of a rabbit snare is to catch rabbits. When the rabbits are caught, the snare is forgotten. The purpose of the word is to convey ideas. When the ideas are grasped, the words are forgotten. Where can I find a man who has forgotten words? He is the one I would like to talk to.[7]

Words find their meaning in times of silence. And yet, it is difficult for us to quiet ourselves and practice silence.

Despite the command for us to be still and know that he is God (Ps 46:10), silence within modern worship services has become filled with negative implications. All too often silence is seen as "too liturgical" and therefore eliminated from the corporate gathering. In the media driven, television production culture in which we currently live, silence is to be avoided and is even termed "dead time." That doesn't sound very encouraging! The busyness of our lives, the hectic pace of our schedules, the intensity

---

5. Nouwen, *Way of the Heart*, 38–39.

6. Nouwen, *Way of the Heart*, 40.

7. Merton, *Way of Chuang Tzu*, 154.

of our personalities saturate our lives on a daily basis and make their way into our times of worship.

It is a good thing for church leaders to teach the congregation how to use silence as part of the worship service. Or if you're a small-group leader or teach a Bible study you too can lead people in a brief time of silence leading into prayer. It's not enough for leaders to suggest people try the discipline of silence on their own (they probably won't do it)—they need to be shown how by guiding them in experiences in God's presence.

The first step is for ministry leaders to practice the discipline of silence in their own personal worship to learn by experience how to deal with the distractions and inner conflicts that may surface. When introducing silence to the community it's good to briefly explain what is happening and why. Helping the congregation understand it is normal if they feel awkward, restless, or have wandering thoughts is the responsibility of church leaders. Explain to the congregation that they are training their minds and bodies to be fully present to the Lord who is fully present to them.

Embracing times of silence and meditation in worship allows God the opportunity to speak. Much of what else we do in worship is directed toward God. Yet in every element of worship, there should not only be opportunities for response, but also aspects of revelation. Being still is primarily the time to allow God to be the communicator as we do nothing else but listen to and focus upon his voice. I am convinced that what we have to say about God is not nearly as important as what God has to say about himself. As we hear from God we open ourselves to the opportunity to be transformed by the renewing of our minds (Rom 12:2). Within stillness, we unclutter ourselves so God can form us from within in a way that only he can.

CONSIDER THIS

Try to clear your mind and sit in silence for ten minutes. Allow God to speak to you. This is not a time to offer supplications (requests), thanksgivings, or intercessions. This is a time to "do nothing." Let God be the doer. It will be hard at first since we are used to "doing." It may take you a few attempts before you succeed. Don't give up.

Next, for those planning worship services, try incorporating a time of meditation in your congregational worship service. Start small—ask the congregation to reflect on a Scripture passage for thirty seconds, asking God to reveal himself through the Scripture. Then conclude the time by singing a song based on the same theme.

FOR FURTHER CONSIDERATION

Morgan, Robert J. *Reclaiming the Lost Art of Biblical Meditation: Find True Peace in Jesus*. Nashville: Nelson, 2017.
Nouwen, Henri J. M. *The Way of the Heart: Connecting with God Through Prayer, Wisdom, and Silence*. New York: Seabury, 1981.

8

Giving as an Act of Worship

I [Paul] have received full payment, and more. I am well supplied, having received from Epaphroditus the gifts you sent, a fragrant offering, a sacrifice acceptable and pleasing to God.

—Philippians 4:18

Giving is oftentimes the most difficult act of worship to offer, especially when it comes to financial giving. At one point in my ministry, I was let go from a church position because the senior pastor wanted to go a different direction with the ministry of the church and felt like I did not fit with that direction. It was a very difficult time for my family; emotionally, spiritually, and financially. Not only did we have to leave our church family, which had ramifications of its own, but we also did not have the paycheck from my job, which we depended upon. I had recently completed my doctoral work, and to top it off, we had just purchased a new home, closing escrow two weeks before being let go.

Amid this storm in our lives, my wife and I agreed that it was important for us to tithe regularly. Although our lives seemed to be in chaos, we knew that God was still sovereign, and we determined that our worship would not be dependent upon our circumstances, but upon God. My family's commitment to worship by means of the giving of our finances, during a time of struggle, no matter how small, was a commitment to God and a testimony to others that our trust in God is unwavering.

Do God's people trust him with their finances only in the good times when it is easy to do so, or do they also trust him when it feels like nothing is going right? For my wife and I, this difficult time was an opportunity for us to live out our faith in ways we had only talked about, and echo Job's declaration, in a small way, that the Lord gives and the Lord takes away; blessed be the name of the Lord (Job 1:21)! As the ushers walked forward down the aisles to prepare to collect the tithes and offerings, my wife would look at me, smile, take out the checkbook and fill in the amount of our giving. We didn't know if we could financially make it through the rest of the week, but we were determined to be faithful to God, knowing he would be faithful to us. He was . . . and is. We never went without food on the table, and we were able to make the mortgage payment each month—a miracle in and of itself. Through the act of giving, especially during our financially challenged time, God revealed himself and continued to prove his faithfulness.

The purpose for me sharing this personal story is not to receive accolades for doing what is good or right. I share this as a reminder that it is God who is good and constantly faithful. He is the initiator of our every act of worship, desiring a right response from us regardless of the present situation of our lives.

❖ ❖ ❖

Almighty God, entirely self-sufficient and requiring no gift from us to sustain him in any way, is not "served by human hands, as though he needed anything" (Acts 17:25). Anything we can give to God is woefully insufficient compared to his abundant riches. Yet God is honored and pleased when we enact a spirit of generosity.

Throughout Scripture we see that the act of giving is a form of worship:

- In the Old Testament, sacrifices to the Lord were designated as "gifts" (Num 18:11).

- When the Magi worshiped Jesus, their devotion was manifested in the form of "gifts" (Matt 2:11).

- A woman, from a point of brokenness and surrender, approached Jesus with an alabaster jar of perfume. She opened the jar and poured the perfume on Jesus's feet. She may have been criticized for "wasting" this expensive perfume, but Jesus saw her gift as an act of worship (Matt 26:6–13).

- It is generally agreed that the "fellowship" mentioned in Acts 2:42 included the act of "giving" (cf. Rom 15:26; 2 Cor 9:13).

- When the church in Philippi gave of their resources for the support of Paul, God considered it "a fragrant offering, a sacrifice acceptable and pleasing to God." (Phil 4:18).

As an act of obedience each Christian must contribute to the work of God. The worshiper must acknowledge that they are but a superintendent of great blessings that God has given them to oversee, contributing generously and cheerfully. In the process of giving, the worshiper should understand that they are the recipients of more than they could ever repay.

Giving is an act of worship that forms the worshiper as they participate in this element of worship. The inclusion of giving as an act of worship within the church worship service is nothing new. Even in the first century we see giving as an important element of worship in the worship gathering. The early Christian apologist Justin Martyr described worship as:

> And on the day called Sunday, all who live in cities or in the country gather together to one place, and the memoirs of the apostles or the writings of the prophets are read, as long as time permits; then, when the reader has ceased, the president verbally instructs and exhorts to the imitation of these good things. Then we all rise together and pray, and as we before said, when our prayer is ended, bread and wine and water are brought, and the president in like manner offers prayers and thanksgivings, according to his ability, and the people assent, saying Amen; and there is a distribution to each, and a participation of that over which thanks have been given, and to those who are absent a portion is sent by the deacons. And they who are well to do, and willing, give what each thinks fit; and what is collected is deposited with the president, who succours the orphans and widows, and those who, through sickness or any other cause, are in want, and those who are in bonds, and the strangers sojourning among us, and in a word takes care of all who are in need.[1]

Church members "gave" as part of worship. They cared for the orphans, widows, the sick, even strangers—all who were in need.

And yet, as we have already seen, worship through giving did not begin with the early church, but occurred regularly throughout Scripture. In Philippians 4:10–20 for example, the apostle Paul writes:

1. Martyr, *First and Second Apologies*, 92–93.

I rejoiced in the Lord greatly that now at length you have revived your concern for me. You were indeed concerned for me, but you had no opportunity. Not that I am speaking of being in need, for I have learned in whatever situation I am to be content. I know how to be brought low, and I know how to abound. In any and every circumstance, I have learned the secret of facing plenty and hunger, abundance and need. I can do all things through him who strengthens me. Yet it was kind of you to share my trouble. And you Philippians yourselves know that in the beginning of the gospel, when I left Macedonia, no church entered into partnership with me in giving and receiving, except you only. Even in Thessalonica you sent me help for my needs once and again. Not that I seek the gift, but I seek the fruit that increases to your credit. I have received full payment, and more. I am well supplied, having received from Epaphroditus the gifts you sent, a fragrant offering, a sacrifice acceptable and pleasing to God. And my God will supply every need of yours according to his riches in glory in Christ Jesus. To our God and Father be glory forever and ever. Amen.

The Philippians showed their love to him through their generosity and Paul's reaction to this voluntary gift included praise to God: "I rejoiced in the Lord greatly" (Phil 4:10). He adds "it was kind of you to share my trouble" (Phil 4:14). Paul rejoiced in the Lord and was thankful. He celebrated because the people of God gathered together as the church in Philippi demonstrated genuine love and faith that "increased to [their] credit" (Phil 4:17).

However, Paul was not finished. Not only did he "rejoice in the Lord greatly" (Phil 4:10), but he also recognized the gift as "a fragrant offering, a sacrifice acceptable and pleasing to God" (Phil 4:18). The Philippians gave to Paul, to support his ministry and in doing so, the Scripture says they offered a sacrifice, acceptable and pleasing to God. This act of giving is acceptable worship to God. Gordon Fee says:

> The imagery is that of the burnt offering, which was understood as a fragrant offering to God. The picture is that of the aroma of the sacrificial fire wafting heavenward—into God's "nostrils," as it were. Properly offered, it becomes "an acceptable sacrifice, pleasing to him." This, Paul says, is what their gift has amounted to from the divine perspective.[2]

---

2. Fee, *Philippians*, 191.

The gift of the church in Philippi, which had met Paul's material needs, pleased God. Giving voluntarily, generously, joyfully, and sacrificially is the type of worship God accepts and that which pleases him.

In her book *The Worship Architect*, Constance Cherry encourages us with these words on offering as an act of worship:

> Scripturally speaking, the offering is always viewed as a response of gratitude to God. In the early church, the offering consisted of gifts for the poor, the widows, and the orphans. The offering is not just a practical matter of taking care of business; it is an act of worship. Because the offering is a gesture offered to God, the manner in which the offering is presented is important to consider. A recommended sequence of worship acts is (1) the offertory sentence (a brief statement or Scripture verse), (2) the collection, (3) the presentation of gifts (a climactic movement), (4) the prayer or song of dedication.[3]

The way in which church leadership and the congregation views the act of giving within the context of the worship service dictates how this element of worship will occur. Is the time of offering in the service seen as an act of worship or is it seen as a necessary action in order to keep the lights on and the staff paid? Dr. Cherry again challenges us,

> In the interest of creating seeker-friendly services, many churches have neglected the offering as a corporate act in favor of locating boxes near the back of the church to receive money. Here is another instance where theology drives practice. If one views the offering as merely taking care of paying the bills, a box at the back would suffice. But if one views the offering as a corporate act of worship with God as the true recipient of our gifts, the offering must be collected, presented, and dedicated to God.[4]

Within many African American worship gatherings, for example, the giving of tithes and offerings is a high point in the worship service. In many churches, the offering plate is placed on a table in the front and the entire congregation processes forward to present their gifts. This approach makes the offering more participatory and provides a time for a joyful giving experience.

Yet giving encompasses more than just the giving of financial resources. Worship involves the act of giving up self in order to do the will

---

3. Cherry, *Worship Architect*, 283–84.
4. Cherry, *Worship Architect*, 284.

of God. In Romans 15:16, it is clear that Paul sees his missionary work among the gentiles as an act of worship through giving. Furthermore, he considers his overall work to be a priestly service of offering up the people as an acceptable sacrifice to God:

> I appeal to you therefore, brothers, by the mercies of God, to present your bodies as a living sacrifice, holy and acceptable to God, which is your spiritual worship. Do not be conformed to this world, but be transformed by the renewal of your mind, that by testing you may discern what is the will of God, what is good and acceptable and perfect. For by the grace given to me I say to everyone among you not to think of himself more highly than he ought to think, but to think with sober judgment, each according to the measure of faith that God has assigned. (Rom 12:1–3)

Although it is not the motivation behind our giving, Scripture is clear that giving blesses the giver. Jesus himself communicated this when he said, "Give and it shall be given to you. A good measure, pressed down, shaken together and running over, will be poured into your lap. For the measure you use, it will be measured to you" (Luke 6:38, NIV). Similarly, the apostle Paul writes to the church in Corinth, "Remember this: whoever sows sparingly will also reap sparingly, and whoever sows generously will also reap generously" (2 Cor 9:6, NIV). The same teaching is found in Ecclesiastes 11:1: "Be generous, and someday you will be rewarded" (CEV).[5] While the specific "reward" or blessing is not stated, what is understood is the spiritual notion of reciprocity—generosity and kindness given always return to us in some way. As Saint Francis of Assisi reminds us, "it is in giving that we receive."[6]

We do not give in order to receive a greater reward. That would be selfish and we must strive to protect ourselves from narcissistic oriented worship. We give because it is within these various forms of giving which the disciple of Jesus experiences a renewed and transformed life, becoming as the very nature of Christ, as Jesus himself, who gave his life as an act of worship to the Father.

5. Scripture taken from the Contemporary English Version. Copyright © 1991, 1992, 1995 by American Bible Society. Used by permission. All rights reserved.

6. The Prayer of St. Francis: Lord, make me an instrument of your peace. Where there is hatred, let me bring love. Where there is offense, let me bring pardon. Where there is discord, let me bring union. Where there is error, let me bring truth. Where there is doubt, let me bring faith. Where there is despair, let me bring hope. Where there is darkness, let me bring your light. Where there is sadness, let me bring joy. O Master, let me not seek as much to be consoled as to console, to be understood as to understand, to be loved as to love, for it is in giving that one receives, it is in self-forgetting that one finds, it is in pardoning that one is pardoned, it is in dying that one is raised to eternal life. Amen.

CONSIDER THIS

To encourage thoughtful engagement in the giving of tithes and offerings, rather than delivering the prayer for the offering from the platform, invite each person in the congregation to offer a silent prayer over his or her offering before it is collected. Then bring everyone back together by placing a corporate prayer on the screen and invite everyone to pray the prayer together.

More than just money: The giving of more than just money was a regular occurrence in the early church as they would share their possessions with one another. On a preplanned Sunday, in addition to the giving of financial tithes and offerings, encourage your congregation to give food to be distributed to the poor in the community. Announce this in advance so they know which Sunday to bring the items. Make this an act of worship within the service, asking the congregation to walk their offerings to baskets in the front of the sanctuary. A congregational song could be sung as the people come forward and a doxology could be sung to conclude the giving time dedicating the offerings to the Lord.

FOR FURTHER CONSIDERATION

Stott, John, and Chris Wright. *The Grace of Giving: Money and the Gospel*. Peabody: Hendrickson, 2016.

9

Baptism as an Act of Worship

> When the goodness and loving kindness of God our Savior appeared, he saved us, not because of works done by us in righteousness, but according to his own mercy, by the washing of regeneration and renewal of the Holy Spirit, whom he poured out on us richly through Jesus Christ our Savior, so that being justified by his grace we might become heirs according to the hope of eternal life.
>
> —Titus 3:4–7

For the first two decades of my life I attended a conservative evangelical church and was raised with the beliefs and values taught in that church. Moreover, right and wrong were clearly defined. The old saying, "Don't smoke, drink, or chew, or go with girls that do" may sound strict, but that was my upbringing and I was regularly reminded of these rules.

I did, however, push the boundaries during my teen years by growing out my hair (a bigger deal for those in my church than you might think) and dating girls that did not attend church (a strict taboo). For someone who grew up in church and was heavily involved in church activities, these were big issues—not necessarily for my family, but for some in my church.

Growing up in a church like this left me with a strong desire to have my understanding of worship stretched in profound ways. As a college student studying Scripture and reading books about the biblical foundations of worship, I began to see there was more to worshiping God than I had previously believed. I came to consider communion to be more than just a remembrance of a past event, prayer more than just supplication and requests, and baptism more than just a command to be obeyed. I began to desire participation in worship gatherings that offered a deeper worship experience than what I had experienced in my younger years. Over the years, I have met others who have gone through similar changes of appreciating and longing for more profound, dare I say, liturgical worship experiences. Author Robert Webber shares why many evangelicals have been attracted to the liturgical church in his book "Evangelicals on the Canterbury Trail" while Todd Hunter shares about his draw to the Anglican Church in "The Accidental Anglican." These two men spent most of their lives in Protestant, free-church traditions and were drawn to the practices of high liturgy. This is not to say that I decided to become an Anglican. I did not. I have, however, gained an appreciation for liturgical worship practices over the years.

A few years ago, I attended a weeklong training on worship and spiritual formation during which the corporate worship times were held in the sanctuary of an Episcopal church. In this church, there was a font filled with water in which the people dipped their fingers and then made the sign of the cross upon themselves as they entered the sanctuary in preparation for meeting with God. This is something not always found in a conservative evangelical church. The leadership in such churches may even have an acute distaste for such an act. I was, however, curious. Therefore I decided that during that week, every time I walked into the sanctuary, I would dip my finger in the font, touch my finger to my forehead and make the symbol of the cross. I wanted to experience why this action was significant to so many Christ-followers around the globe.

What I discovered surprised me. As I dipped my finger into the font I felt the wetness of the water and was reminded of my baptism as a young child. I remembered entering the water in my swimming trunks, feeling cold and wet. When I touched my wet finger to my forehead, I remembered being immersed in the water as a symbol of death and being brought up out of the water as a symbol of new life. While I made the symbol of the cross I was reminded that my baptism was done in the name of the triune God, Father, Son, and Holy Spirit, and in light of Christ's atoning work on the cross.

I did this each time I entered the sanctuary, some fifteen times that week, wondering if doing it so many times would diminish the impact.

The repetition did not. In fact, as I continued to do this, the action became more powerful. I was personally deeply impacted, feeling as though I was being drawn to a deeper understanding of the triune God. My actions were thus a visible sign of a vow to become more like Jesus. This repetitive act provided a fresh renewal of my baptism and vows and a forceful reminder of my spiritual death and resurrection in Christ.

❖ ❖ ❖

Baptism, as understood by the church tradition in which I was raised, is an important step for each Christ-follower as an outward declaration of an inward faith. Yet, I have often wondered if those who journey through the waters of baptism are truly changed on the inside as a result of what God is doing through this element of worship. Too often I have seen professing Christ-followers obey Christ's command of baptism only to walk away from the church and seemingly the faith a short time later. Cyril of Jerusalem, distinguished theologian of the early church, shared the same concern about baptism of bodies but not hearts.[1] So, what inward experiences should be expected from those who are baptized?

First and foremost, baptism is about identity. We find our identity—who we are in Christ Jesus—through baptism. When we are baptized, we are incorporated into Christ's life and his body—the church. Through baptism we come to realize that we are in a drama that is not our own. To say it another way, we did not write the script. My sons' baptisms illustrated this for me. As their father, I had the special privilege of participating in both of their baptisms. As I stood in the water with them, it was my hands that guided their bodies under and up out of the water; but I was very aware that I was participating in a script that God wrote. Their baptisms outwardly revealed the inward work God had performed in their lives. In this sense baptism is a symbolic act of worship.

Through baptism, God confirms our identity as we become more like Christ. And for those who have previously been baptized and are observers of someone else's baptism, the worshiper should remember their own baptism allowing God to refresh the sign and seal of regeneration upon their own lives. Spiritual formation through baptism should continue to occur instead of being a one-time occurrence.

Spiritually formative, transforming elements that occur through baptism include:

---

1. Cyril, *Lectures on the Christian Sacraments*, 40–41.

- Washing/Renewing (Acts 22:16; 1 Cor 6:11; Eph 5:27; Titus 3:5)

- Transferring (1 Cor 12:13; Gal 6:15,16; Acts 26:18; Col 1:12–13; Titus 2:11)

- Naming (1 Cor 1:13, 15; Gal 3:26, 29; Rev 2:17; 3:12)

- Sealing (Rom 4:11; Eph 1:13; 4:30; 2 Tim 2:19)

- Uniting (Rom 6)

- Disrobing/Robing (Gal 3:27; Eph 4:20–32; Col 3)

Baptism is a sign and seal of our renewed life in Christ. As a sign it points beyond itself to the greater reality of Christ's redemptive work and as a seal it conveys the guarantee of God's grace to us through Jesus Christ. In the New Testament we find that baptism is a sign of rebirth. In Titus 3:5 Paul calls baptism "the water of rebirth" and in John 3:5 Jesus speaks of being "born again by water and the Spirit." In our baptism the regeneration that we have in Christ is declared, demonstrated, promised, and sealed.

We see symbols of baptism throughout Scripture, both in the Old and New Testaments. One of the first times we see the symbol of baptism in Scripture is with Noah and the flood. Centuries after the flood, Peter tells his listeners,

> [Christ] went and proclaimed to the spirits in prison because they formerly did not obey, when God's patience waited in the days of Noah, while the ark was being prepared, in which a few, that is, eight persons, were brought safely through water. Baptism, which corresponds to this, now saves you, not as a removal of dirt from the body but as an appeal to God for a good conscience, through the resurrection of Jesus Christ. (1 Pet 3:19–21)

The word "corresponds" that Paul uses here is in relation to Noah's flood and includes:

1. Escaping through drowning waters: Just as Noah and his family escaped death from flooding waters by means of God's provision of an ark, so Christians today escape death from sin by means of God's provision of redeeming grace through Jesus, our Savior.

2. A colony of sole survivors: Because of God's great mercy, Noah and his family—Noah's wife, three sons and their wives—were the sole survivors of God's wrath and judgement. Christians today, because of God's great mercy through the sacrifice of Jesus Christ, will be the sole

survivors of God's wrath and judgement, receiving eternal life. Those who do not put their faith in Jesus Christ will receive their punishment of eternal death.

3. The survivors establishing God's new humanity: Noah and his family, eight individuals in all,[2] were the whole of humanity after the flood. They were to "be fruitful and multiply" (Gen 1:28) in order to repopulate the earth. Christians are God's new humanity in Christ and will be the exclusive population of the new heavens and new earth (Rev 21:1).

The Old Testament exodus is also a symbol for baptism. "For I do not want you to be unaware, brethren, that our fathers were all under the cloud and all passed through the sea; and all were baptized into Moses in the cloud and in the sea" (1 Cor 10:1–2). Paul is providing a Christological interpretation of the exodus account; he is making the connection between the exodus from Egypt and salvation in Christ. For the people of Israel, during the time of the exodus, there were two primary substitutes in death. First, the Passover lambs served as substitutes as the blood placed over the doorposts of the dwellings of the Israelites served as a substitute in death when the angel of death passed over them. In the same way, the blood of Jesus shed on the cross is placed over our lives, resulting in eternal death passing us by. On their journey out of Egypt, Egyptians served as substitutes for the Israelites as the waters of the Red Sea came crashing down around the pursuing Egyptian army. Correspondingly, as we go through the waters of baptism our old selves are sacrificed and we become new creations in Christ.

Furthermore, in both the exodus and baptism, there is a crossing of death's boundary. As the Israelites journey through the Red Sea, with the waters on both sides, they come out the other side a delivered people. In the same way, when we rise out of the waters in baptism,[3] we can be confident of the new creation we have become.

2. The number eight in the Bible represents new beginning, or new creation. God saved eight people to provide a new beginning following the flood.

3. The forms or modes of baptism include immersion, in which the entire body is submerged into a body of water (Mark 1:10); affusion, in which a substantial amount of water is poured on the head (Acts 2:17, 33); and sprinkling, in which a small amount of water is sprinkled on the head (Num 8:6–13; Exod 24:8). All three represent biblical and longstanding historical practices. Some traditions feel strongly that immersion is the proper form because the Greek word for baptism, *baptizo*, can be translated "dip" or "immerse." While Scripture reveals that when Jesus was baptized, he came "up out of the water," some may claim that if he was standing waist-high in the water he could still come "up out of the water." As a result, baptismal modes seem to fall into two categories:

One further instance of Old Testament baptismal symbolism is the crossing through the Jordan River. The symbolism to baptism is similar to that of the crossing of the Red Sea but with one primary difference. In the first instance, the Red Sea crossing was immediate deliverance from slavery in Egypt, and in the latter instance, the Jordan crossing was immediate deliverance into the rest of the Promised Land. Both correspond to baptism and the new life we find in Christ.

In our baptism we turn from sin and accept God's invitation to join his forever family, becoming joint heirs with Jesus (Rom 8:14–17). This gives the baptized a new identity as a new creation in Christ, "sharing in his new humanity, set free from sin and death by his death on the cross, risen with him to eternal life, and ascended with him to the heights of glory and honor."[4] As seen, within the New Testament, the image of the blood of the Passover sacrifice and Feast (Jesus is the Passover sacrifice in 1 Corinthians 5:7) appears in direct correlation with the water of the Red Sea (and with the water of the Jordan River). So while blood atones, or provides deliverance from the condemnation of sin, water in the New Testament provides for eternal life, or the deliverance into the rest (or peace) of heaven.

In looking at Jesus's baptism itself, Pastor Leonard J. Vander Zee reflects upon the fact that all three synoptic Gospels point out that the heavens were opened with God's favor and blessing as God poured out his love upon the world. A correlation is made to the prophet Isaiah, who centuries before cried out, "O that you would rend the heavens and come down" (Isa 64:1). At Jesus's baptism, God does just that. Vander Zee states, "The opening of the heavens . . . declares to us that in Christ all the spiritual blessings of heaven are now available to all who are united with Christ in baptism . . . At Christ's baptism and at ours, God opens heaven's door to us in grace. We now have peace with God through Christ and in the Spirit, inviting us to commune with him in prayer and worship him in purity of spirit."[5] Baptism unites us in Christ's death and resurrection, as Paul makes clear in his letter to the church in Rome:

---

those who immerse only (primarily Anabaptists, Baptists, Churches of Christ/Christian Churches, and others generally from the Free Church movement) and those who practice any of the three modes in order to baptize (primarily Lutheran, Reformed, and Wesleyan traditions).

4. Vander Zee, *Christ, Baptism and the Lord's Supper*, 109.

5. Vander Zee, *Christ, Baptism and the Lord's Supper*, 82.

What shall we say then? Are we to continue in sin that grace may abound? By no means! How can we who died to sin still live in it? Do you not know that all of us who have been baptized into Christ Jesus were baptized into his death? We were buried therefore with him by baptism into death, in order that, just as Christ was raised from the dead by the glory of the Father, we too might walk in newness of life.

For if we have been united with him in a death like his, we shall certainly be united with him in a resurrection like his. We know that our old self was crucified with him in order that the body of sin might be brought to nothing, so that we would no longer be enslaved to sin. For one who has died has been set free from sin. Now if we have died with Christ, we believe that we will also live with him. We know that Christ, being raised from the dead, will never die again; death no longer has dominion over him. For the death he died he died to sin, once for all, but the life he lives he lives to God. So you also must consider yourselves dead to sin and alive to God in Christ Jesus. (Rom 6:1–11)

It is in this text that we find the concise meaning of baptism in the New Testament. Yet, it is not a simple explanation as it shows us that the New Testament church was also struggling with a serious issue of sin and forgiveness. Many in the church had taken hold of the idea that "grace abounds," believing they could sin as much as they wanted because God would faithfully forgive. And though God is faithful to forgive, Paul challenges the believers in Rome by telling them they are wrong in this thinking. Why? Because they were "baptized into Christ Jesus." Paul makes it clear that spiritual formation is occurring during baptism and that those baptized should live lives that are changed by Christ. In other words, they should live baptized lives.

When I was a doctoral student, I had the opportunity to participate in two baptismal renewals. The first occurred during a worship service led by other students at the school. The students led the congregation in a time of worship focused on the remembrance of our baptisms. Near the end of the service, students began walking around the sanctuary flicking water from birch branches over the congregation. As the water droplets splashed upon my face, God reminded me of my baptism. Surprisingly, this action was extremely effective in helping me remember my baptism as a young boy.

The second experience occurred as an exercise in one of my classes. Members of the class were invited to stand around a baptismal font in a small chapel. We were then encouraged to come forward and participate in renewing our baptismal vows. It was a powerful experience for me as I approached the water to remember my baptism. However, that was not what made the worship experience so powerful. What made it powerful was the class celebrating our baptisms together as the body of Christ and seeing God move in and through each person gathered around the font. Some simply dipped their finger in the water and then touched their forehead. Others touched the water and then rubbed their eyes, ears, mouth, etc., recommitting their entire self to the Lord. One member of the class even began to splash the water, causing it to overflow out of the bowl. I will remember that time for the rest of my life because God did a spiritual work within me—shaping, molding, and forming me through baptism.

The concluding prayer from a liturgy of baptismal renewal reminds us of this spiritually formative work of the Spirit.

> Eternal Father, your mighty acts of salvation have been made known through water—from the moving of your Spirit upon the waters of creation, to the deliverance of your people through the flood and through the Red Sea. In the fullness of time you sent Jesus, nurtured in the water of a womb, baptized by John, and anointed by your Spirit. He called his disciples to share in the baptism of his death and resurrection and to make disciples of all nations. Pour out your Holy Spirit, and by this gift of water call to our remembrance the grace declared to us in our baptism. For you have washed away our sins, and you clothe us with righteousness throughout our lives, that dying and rising with Christ we may share in his final victory. Amen.

In baptism, it is not enough to simply get wet; as we do when we bathe, which should be a regular occurrence in our lives to cleanse our external body. Baptism, on the other hand, includes a cleansing of our inner being with spiritually formative consequences. This is the work of the Spirit through baptism. It is not enough to baptize the body, there must also be a baptism of the heart.

CONSIDER THIS

Are there ways for you to help your congregation remember their baptism? It could be planning a worship service that focuses on baptism renewal, or asking your congregation to reflect upon their baptism as a video is played in a worship service, or creating an artistic display in the lobby or sanctuary with water and Scripture to help people recall their baptism.

FOR FURTHER CONSIDERATION

Stookey, Laurence H. *Baptism: Christ's Act in the Church*. Nashville: Abingdon, 1982.

10

Other Acts of Worship

And whatever you do, whether in word or deed, do it all in the name of the
Lord Jesus, giving thanks to God the Father through him.

—COLOSSIANS 3:17

FROM THE BEGINNING OF the worship service to the end, biblical Christian
worship offers us an active role in rehearsing the story of God. In addition
to the elements of the worship service already considered throughout this
book, additional worship elements assist the congregation in their right
response to God's revelations.

While God doesn't prescribe a specific form of worship in his word,
he does give us guidelines to follow as we gather in his name. Paul's first
letter to the Corinthians gives us a few examples to consider: "When you
come together, each one has a hymn, a lesson, a revelation, a tongue, or an
interpretation. Let all things be done for building up" (1 Cor 14:26). When
Christians gather for public worship, one goal is to edify, or build up, one
another in the faith through the proclamation of the word of God through
various elements of worship. Paul continues with another guideline for
public worship in his instructions to the Corinthians: "all things should be
done decently and in order" (1 Cor 14:40). This guideline goes along with
the first because if things are disorderly in a worship service, it is far more
difficult for a believer to follow along and be edified. Also, it may give the
wrong impression of believers and of God to those outside the church, "for

God is not a God of confusion but of peace" (1 Cor 14:33). Therefore, a public worship service will incisively gather in an orderly way with the goal of building up the church.

So let's consider other acts of worship within a worship service and how they aid in forming the worshiper.

PREPARATION

It is important for us to take time before a worship service begins to quiet ourselves and to prepare to hear from God. If we are to allow our life and worship of God to intersect, it is important that we pay attention to our movement from who we are and what we need, to being ready and prepared to hear from God through his word. Every act of preparation should help move us into worship—into the story of God at work.

There are many forces that are vying for our attention, not only during the week, but even as we actively prepare our hearts for worship with others; the stress of work, discipling children, caring for aging parents, worrying about medical insurance, and the list goes on. As we prepare to enter into corporate worship, we must take time to prepare well and invite God to begin to form us even in this time of preparation.

CALL TO WORSHIP

The overall purpose of the call to worship is not only to begin the worship service, but to help the people of God gather into a distinct community of worshipers. As we gather, we need time to focus ourselves, to settle down inwardly, to remember who God is, who we are, and why we have gathered. It is for this reason that I like to use Scripture as a call to worship.

Utilizing Scripture as a call to worship immediately takes the focus off the worshiper and places it on God. When we hear the word of the Lord as the first thing in the service, we are reminded that it is God who initiates worship and it is he that we have come to worship.

Scripture Examples

Jeremiah 9:23–24

> This is what the LORD says:
> "Let not the wise man boast of his wisdom or the strong man boast of his strength or the rich man boast of his riches, but let him who boasts boast about this: that he understands and knows me, that I am the LORD, who exercises kindness, justice and righteousness on earth, for in these I delight," declares the LORD.

We are here this morning to boast in God. Let's not hold back, but join together in worship with all our heart, soul, mind, and strength.

Psalm 95:1–3

Welcome. This morning, let the Psalmist remind us of why we have gathered together and whom we are here to worship.

> Oh come, let us sing to the Lord; let us make a joyful noise to the rock of our salvation! Let us come into his presence with thanksgiving; let us make a joyful noise to him with songs of praise! For the Lord is a great God, and a great King above all gods.

Psalm 57:7–11

> My heart is steadfast, O God, my heart is steadfast; I will sing and make music. Awake, my soul! Awake, harp and lyre! I will awaken the dawn. I will praise you, O Lord, among the nations; I will sing of you among the peoples. For great is your love, reaching to the heavens; your faithfulness reaches to the skies. Be exalted, O God, above the heavens; let your glory be over all the earth.

Leading the call to worship as a responsive reading of Scripture is also effective as it places the words of God upon the lips of his people at the start of the service.

Responsive Reading Examples

Psalm 99

LEADER:
The Lord reigns, let the nations tremble; he sits enthroned between the cherubim, let the earth shake.
CONGREGATION:
Great is the Lord in Zion; he is exalted over all the nations.
LEADER:
Let them praise your great and awesome name—
CONGREGATION:
He is holy.
LEADER:
The King is mighty, he loves justice—you have established equity;
CONGREGATION:
in Jacob you have done what is just and right.
LEADER:
Exalt the Lord our God and worship at his footstool;
CONGREGATION:
He is holy.
LEADER:
Moses and Aaron were among his priests, Samuel was among those who called on his name; they called on the Lord and he answered them.
CONGREGATION:
He spoke to them from the pillar of cloud; they kept his statutes and the decrees he gave them.
LEADER:
Lord our God, you answered them; you were to Israel a forgiving God, though you punished their misdeeds.
CONGREGATION:
Exalt the Lord our God and worship at his holy mountain, for the Lord our God is holy.

Psalm 36:5–9

LEADER:
Your love, Lord, reaches to the heavens . . .
CONGREGATION:

your faithfulness to the skies.
LEADER:
Your righteousness is like the highest mountains,
CONGREGATION:
your justice like the great deep.
LEADER:
You, Lord, preserve both people and animals.
CONGREGATION:
How priceless is your unfailing love, O God!
LEADER:
People take refuge in the shadow of your wings.
CONGREGATION:
They feast on the abundance of your house;
LEADER:
you give them drink from your river of delights.
CONGREGATION:
For with you is the fountain of life; in your light we see light.

GREETING ONE ANOTHER/PASSING OF THE PEACE

Paul began nearly every one of his letters with a greeting of peace (Rom 1:7; 1 Cor 1:3; Gal 1:3; Eph 1:2; Phil 1:2; 1 Thess 1:1; 2 Thess 1:2; 1 Tim 1:2; 2 Tim 1:2; Titus 1:4; Phlm 1:3, and more). This was not an insincere expression of peace, but a deep-rooted offer of peace founded in Christ. In early church worship gatherings it was appropriate to offer the kiss of peace after the prayers. The kiss is mentioned several places in the New Testament (Rom 16:16; 1 Pet 5:14; 1 Cor 16:20; 2 Cor 13:12) and was a gesture signifying peace between God and his people through his Holy Spirit. In the ancient church, it was an actual kiss. It was not a sexual act in any way, but was an intimate, common greeting among friends. This is still the case in many cultures today. I can remember being kissed on both cheeks, though sometimes on the lips, and most often by men, when I was in Russia doing ministry in churches. For them this was a friendly greeting with spiritual implications.

It was also a way for the early church to remind one another, during a time of severe persecution, that Christ's peace was available to all who seek him. In support of this practice, we read in the second-century testimony of Justin Martyr that there is a kiss present within the worship of the early Christians:

"Having ended the prayers, we salute one another with a kiss. There is then brought to the president of the brethren bread and a cup of wine" (*First Apology*, 65)

In the *Apostolic Tradition* (third century), Hippolytus comments on the liturgical practice of greeting one another with a kiss:

"After the catechumens have finished praying, they do not give the kiss of peace, for their kiss is not yet pure. But the faithful shall greet one another with a kiss, men with men, and women with women. Men must not greet women with a kiss."

Today, the peace of Christ is still an added benefit to any worship service. The kiss of peace, or sometimes simply called "Pax" or "Peace," is often practiced by hugging or shaking hands while saying "the peace of Christ be with you" or some such modification. Yet there are many Protestant churches today that have altered this action to be more of an intermittent practice, essentially serving as a break in the worship of the church in order to talk with friends and meet visitors to the church. This "meet and greet" time in the service becomes somewhat of an obligatory action and is often dreaded by those who do not consider themselves extroverts, as it potentially becomes filled with shallow interactions, also called "small talk." However, the traditional kiss of peace was a sober and purposeful liturgical act for worshipers. In the traditions that practiced it, it was supposed to be a holy greeting that both symbolized and created unity and reconciliation in the body of Christ.

Therefore, for the church today, instead of a simple exhortation to "greet one another," we should be encouraging worshipers to pass the peace with a handshake or an embrace, while saying, with a real sense of warmth and love, "The peace of Christ be with you." It is also important to encourage worshipers to not only offer Christ's peace but to receive the peace of the Lord over their lives and return the offer of peace with the response "and also with you."

Scripture Example (congregational response in italics)

A new command I give you, that you love one another as I have loved you. The peace of Christ be with you all.
And also with you.
Based on John 13:34.

Liturgical Example (congregational response in italics)

The peace of Christ with you.
And also with you.

Contemporary Example

Live in the peace of Christ . . . today and always.

EXHORTATION

Exhortation, like preaching or teaching, is a learned ability. For those God has called to lead worship, he has also called to fulfill all the dynamics of the role that are necessary to provide proper direction for God's people. Exhortation is a way to encourage others toward responding to God through worship. It is neither coercion nor manipulation, but falls into the area of persuasion. Paul wrote, "Therefore, knowing the fear of the Lord, we persuade others" (2 Cor 5:11), and he commanded Titus, "Declare these things; exhort and rebuke with all authority. Let no one disregard you" (Titus 2:15).

Since every aspect of the worship service provides an opportunity for the Spirit of God to form the worshiper, every word spoken in the corporate worship gathering must be purposeful and thoughtful. There is no such thing as expendable words when it comes to worship. Although exhortations may be spontaneous, as God has the ability to do whatever he chooses in whichever way he so chooses, it is highly recommended that the worship leader thoughtfully consider each statement spoken to the congregation; as those words will help persuade others and set the foundation for the Spirit to work within the hearts and lives of the people. Worship leaders often do not plan spoken words of exhortation, not because they wish to rely upon the Holy Spirit, but because of a lack of planning and intentionality. Can not the Almighty omnipresent God that we worship lead our planning in advance? And since all that we do in leading worship is vitally important to the congregation's spiritual formation, wouldn't it be wise for us to consider every aspect of what we do. After all, we are speaking of that which has eternal significance.

Exhortations are offered in a variety of ways and oftentimes are utilized as transitions between other worship elements. For instance, after a prayer and before a song, the worship leader may exhort the congregation with words of encouragement, challenge, or affirmation that echo scriptural truth. At yet another time, in between two songs, the worship leader may ask the congregation to speak out various names of God found throughout Scripture.[1] Additionally, an exhortation exalting God by considering his attributes provides an opportunity for the congregation to think deeply upon God and respond to him in worship. Each exhortation can be used by the Spirit of God to form our inner beings toward Christ-likeness.

DISMISSAL

The dismissal is more than an indicator that the worship service is over. Just like every other act of worship, the dismissal tells a story. It is the conclusion of our gathered worship but the beginning of our service in and to the world. This service continues until the worshipers gather again to worship as the body of Christ. I once heard that every worship service ends with a comma, not a period. With this in mind, the content of the dismissal should be well thought out. Although brief, careful thought needs to be given to the words and actions that send God's people out into the world, where they will continue to "declare the praises of him who called [them] out of darkness into his wonderful light" (1 Pet 2:9). As with the call to worship, I prefer for the words of dismissal, or benediction, to consist of the words of God. In this way, God provides the first and last words of the worship service. After all, his words are much better than anything we can come up with.

Examples

Romans 15:5–6

"May the God of endurance and encouragement grant you to live in such harmony with one another, in accord with Christ Jesus, that together you may with one voice glorify the God and Father of our Lord Jesus Christ."

---

1. With nearly one thousand names and titles of God found throughout Scripture, this should be an attainable exercise for any congregation. Worship leaders and pastors must be prepared to help "prime the pump" by offering a name or two if the congregation is slow in starting, and interjecting when there is a lull. Be sure not to rush this moment and be okay with brief times of silence as your congregation is thinking of various names. The more frequently you do exercises like this, the better your congregation will become at thinking in these ways and speaking out.

Ephesians 3:20–21

"Now to him who is able to do immeasurably more than all we ask or imagine, according to his power that is at work within us, to him be glory in the church and in Christ Jesus throughout all generations, forever and ever!" Amen.

Jude 24 and 25

"To him who is able to keep you from falling and to present you before his glorious presence without fault and with great joy—to the only God our Savior be glory, majesty, power, and authority, through Jesus Christ our Lord, before all ages, now and forevermore!" Amen.

Whether it is the beginning of the service or the end, or any moment in between, every element of worship has the potential to form our lives in a spiritual manner pleasing to the Lord. "Worship not only presents Christ, it causes Christ to be formed in my life. . . . When I am thoroughly involved in worship I not only hear and see, but I become. I am to become God's word and God's bread to the world. To be formed by worship is to take on the characteristics of Christ, to be shaped by his presence within."[2] As we worship, may we sense the Spirit drawing us to the Father by way of the Son.

CONSIDER THIS

For those in freeform church traditions: in your planning of the worship service this week, pick a passage of Scripture that compliments the Scripture text the preacher will be focusing on in the sermon. Once you have the complimentary Scripture chosen, use that passage to design the preparation (on screen, prelude, etc.), call to worship, passing of the peace, exhortations, and dismissal. In other words, string together the Scripture passage throughout the "Other Acts of Worship" in your worship service. This should be in addition to the songs, prayers, and other elements of worship in the service. See if creating a cohesive flow of thought in the worship service provides an opportunity for the congregation to think deeply upon God and open their hearts and minds to the moving of the Holy Spirit in their lives.

2. Webber, *Worship Is a Verb*, 105.

FOR FURTHER CONSIDERATION

Cherry, Constance. *The Worship Architect: A Blueprint for Designing Culturally Relevant and Biblically Faithful Services.* Grand Rapids: Baker Academic, 2010.

The Worship Sourcebook. Grand Rapids: Faith Alive Christian Resources and Calvin Institute of Christian Worship, 2013.

11

Sacred Space and Worship Formation

An altar of earth you shall make for me and sacrifice on it your burnt offerings and your peace offerings, your sheep and your oxen. In every place where I cause my name to be remembered I will come to you and bless you.

—EXODUS 20:24

How lovely is your dwelling place, O Lord of hosts! My soul longs, yes, faints for the courts of the Lord; my heart and flesh sing for joy to the living God. For a day in your courts is better than a thousand elsewhere. I would rather be a doorkeeper in the house of my God than dwell in the tents of wickedness.

—PSALM 84:1–2, 10

I LIVE IN SOUTHERN California. Consequently, within a two-hour drive, I have access to beaches, mountains, deserts, and forests. Whether it is lying on the beach at the Pacific Ocean, hiking the trails of the San Bernardino mountains, riding a motorcycle in the Mojave Desert, or camping in the Angeles National Forest, the scenery is often quite breathtaking. It is in places such as these that I can see the handiwork of God displayed, and I am drawn to worship.

If it's not the sight of God's natural creation that emboldens your worship, it may be a grand cathedral or a small church chapel—those incredibly beautiful architectural creations that inspire awe and wonder.

Oftentimes, when we are in places like nature or a beautiful church sanctuary, we don't even realize we have entered into worship, but there we are, standing in awe saying, whether with actual voices, or just with our hearts, "The heavens declare the glory of God, and the sky above proclaims his handiwork" (Ps 19:1).

A friend of mine created a prayer closet in his house. He would spend an hour in this closet every morning praying for his family, church, friends, the world, and anything else God laid on his heart. It was a simple little room decorated with pillows for kneeling and paper with prayer requests and reminders taped to the walls. It was practical, and a meaningful sacred space for him.

It doesn't matter where you are. The incredible thing about God is that he enjoys hearing from those he loves no matter where they are. He simply asks us to worship.

❖ ❖ ❖

The space in which we offer our worship is critically important because it helps shape the ways in which we are spiritually formed. Worshiping in a large cathedral has the potential of enhancing the idea that God is majestic. Worshiping under a canopy of trees in the mountains may enhance the idea that God is Creator. Worshiping in a small traditional chapel may enhance the idea that God is intimate. Our setting, or space, can definitely shape the way we view God, thereby shaping the way in which we worship.

In the Old Testament we find the story of Jacob and the altar he built for the Lord. One evening as Jacob slept, he dreamed that he saw angels coming and going from heaven on a ladder. God also spoke to Jacob in his dream. When he woke, he said, "Surely the Lord is in this place and I was not aware of it. . . . How awesome is this place!" (Gen 28:16–17). What had been an ordinary place in the desert became sacred because in that place, Jacob experienced God.

In the book of Exodus, before the construction of the tabernacle, there was the tent of meeting, as described in Exodus 33:7–11. The tent of meeting was erected by Moses some distance outside of the Israelite camp, an indicator of the broken fellowship between God and the Israelites after the incident of the golden calf (Exod 32). This was the physical space where God would meet with Moses, and Moses would seek God's guidance. As a result, Moses would probably assume a posture of humbleness, bowing low or kneeling with his face to the ground (*proskuneo*) while in the tent. Though he was the leader of the Israelites, he understood that he was a servant of God.

In the gospels, we read that Jesus took his disciples to the garden of Gethsemane located at the foot of the Mount of Olives (Luke 22:39–46). Luke states in verse 39 that Jesus went, "as was his custom, to the Mount of Olives." The phrase "as was his custom" expresses that this place was probably important or special to Jesus. What drew Jesus to that space on a regular basis? Was it simply a place of solitude away from the potential distractions and needs of the community? Did it remind Jesus of the garden, a sacred space, that his Father established in Eden? Just as Moses separated himself from the camp, Jesus removed himself from the disciples so he could establish a sacred space and come before his Father. Both set their focus on God and humbled themselves before him.

Jacob experienced God in the desert and that place became sacred to him. Moses met with God in the tent of meeting and that place became sacred to him. Jesus conversed with his Father in the garden and that place became sacred to him. In the same way, God is experienced in our churches and those places become sacred to us.

The architectural design of our churches is shaped by our concept of worship, which in turn shapes our worship experience. Architecture has the potential to provide a sacred aesthetic for our worship. Anyone who has visited the grand cathedrals of Europe can attest. The rising spires point heavenward, the ringing bells declare to the community, and the stained glass windows convey the biblical stories. Even the walls, ceilings, furniture, and floors are filled with symbols of the faith. It has been this way for centuries.

Besides the symbolism found in the materials of the tabernacle and temple, we see symbolic art in the catacombs where early Christians would go to escape persecution. On the walls of the catacombs one could see, and in some cases, still see to this day, symbols carved into the walls. The symbolic art depicted various themes of Christianity such as a fish, indicating Christ; a dove, signifying the peace of heaven; an anchor, expressing the firmness of faith; the palm, peacock, and phoenix, among others, referring to eternal salvation. These symbols were placed with the intention of encouraging others in their faith and fostering spiritual formation within.

Pre-Reformation churches were full of symbols—imagery and artwork that helped tell the story of God. The use of symbolic art was vitally important, as a large portion of the population was illiterate. Stained glass windows were sometimes called the "poor man's Bible" because of their depictions of biblical stories. By viewing the imagery one would be encouraged in their spiritual journey toward God.

Many post-Reformation churches were much simpler in design, often devoid of symbolism and ornamentation. Because of the Reformation doctrine of *Sola Scriptura*,[1] there was in many places an increased emphasis on the word spoken through Scripture and sermon with significantly less attention on symbolism. The walls of churches became bare and art forms that had previously been used to depict the story of God were eliminated.

And yet, "Buildings referred to as 'the house of God' or 'the house of worship' should proclaim the excellencies of the One in whose honor they are constructed and in whose name we gather. The second command of the Decalogue, 'you shall not bear the name of YHWH your God in vain,' applies not only to individual believers and to the church as a body, but also to the buildings we have consecrated for worship."[2] Our church buildings, much like our lives, should proclaim the truth of who God is and who he wants to be in our lives.

The way in which our worship space is set up says a lot about what we consider to be the most important element of worship. For instance, the church that positions the baptistry at the front and center of the sanctuary highly values baptism. The church that places the communion table at the front and center highly values eucharist. When the pulpit is positioned at the front and center of the sanctuary, it shows that the church highly values the preaching of God's word through the sermon. And the church that places the musical instruments and the praise band at the center highly values musical worship.

1. *Sola Scriptura* is Latin for "Scripture alone."
2. Block, *For the Glory of God*, 326.

THIS DO IN REMEMBRANCE OF ME

This is not to say that the church that places the baptistry at the center does not value the sermon or musical worship. The placement of articles in the worship space does however often express what is considered to be the most valued element of worship. It is the function of space to promote rather than hinder congregational participation. The way in which we set up our worship space should serve the congregation's worship of God. Often, our church sanctuaries are constructed in ways that do not encourage congregational participation, and in fact, work against this primary function of the gathering space. Daniel Block states, "Structures that bear the brand of the Lord but reflect the materialistic values or chaos of our culture shame the name of Christ."[3] Recently, many of our church sanctuaries have begun to look more like a community theater than a sanctuary. I think it's time we return to letting a church sanctuary be a church sanctuary, a concert venue be a concert venue, a civic center be a civic center, and a movie theater be a movie theater.[4]

Now the Bible makes it clear that God is everywhere:

> Where shall I go from your Spirit? Or where shall I flee from your presence? If I ascend to heaven, you are there! If I make my bed in Sheol, you are there! If I take the wings of the morning and dwell in the uttermost parts of the sea, even there your hand shall lead me, and your right hand shall hold me. (Ps 139:7–10)

Theologians call this omnipresence, being everywhere at once. For most Christians, the sacred derives its meaning and application from Jesus's words in the gospels: "The kingdom of God is in your midst" (Luke 17:21). In other words, the sacred is not limited to a particular space or time. God is always in our midst, ready to be encountered if we would simply pay attention and acknowledge him, which would subsequently make any space sacred.

And yet, though God is omnipresent, the Bible also teaches that God is present in a special way in certain locations. We see this to be true throughout Scripture. Although the metaphor of thin places does not appear in

---

3. Block, *For the Glory of God*, 326.

4. Since the gathering together of the body of Christ is a critical aspect of the church, I would encourage any church to meet together wherever you can, whether or not you have the opportunity to meet in a space designated for worship. If the only space available for your congregation to gather is a rented movie theater, by all means, meet there. I do believe, however, that a church building has the potential to spiritually encourage and form the worshiper's response to God and declare in and of itself that this place is intended for the worship of the Most High God.

Scripture, it is clear that places like the garden of Eden, Mount Sinai, the tabernacle, and the temple, among others, are places that fostered intimacy with God. These were places where people experienced God with more immediacy and intimacy and had life-transforming experiences. There are also places today in which God seems more present than others. These places have recently been termed "thin places." These are places where God's presence seems stronger than any other place. Since the beginning of recorded history, people have been fascinated and drawn to places where the veil between this world and the eternal world is thin—a meeting of heaven and earth. The dividing line between the holy and the ordinary are thin in these places. For some it may be the beach. Others may find God's presence strongest in the mountains. For others, it may be in a backyard garden.

In a blog on thin places, Mark D. Roberts states, "the purpose of thin places is to help us realize that all places can be thin. Or, better yet, perhaps the purpose of a thin place is to train us to make the other places in our lives thinner. Moreover, when we realize that the Spirit of God dwells within us, we will come to believe that we are called to be thin places, as God makes his presence known through us."[5] Just as there are specific places where we sense God more powerfully than others, there are certain people that seem to inspire us in our walk with God more than others. As we spend time with these individuals, we sense God's presence and are encouraged to be better followers of Christ because of their example. They have become a thin place for us as heaven meets earth when we are in their presence. This is a beautiful thing and we should strive to be a thin place for others.

A physical sacred space location is critical in worship but it is not mandatory. We remember that Jesus shattered the preconceived what, where, when, and how of worship as he talked with the woman at the well. It is not the place that makes worship, it is he whom we worship. Yet God understands that as human beings, our surroundings shape us. Within our worship experiences, those surroundings can either enhance or detract. Consequently, God shows that sacred space is valuable as he gives detailed directions for the building of the worship space known as the tabernacle. When reading the book of Exodus, one cannot help but see the importance of sacred space. Of the three important topics of the entire book—the other two being the Exodus and the law—the

5. Roberts, "Thin Places," 2012.

vast majority of the book deals with the tabernacle. Furthermore, God is concerned that Moses construct the tabernacle precisely the way God intended, "Exactly as I show you concerning the pattern of the tabernacle, and of all its furniture, so you shall make it" (Exod 25:9). Moses was ordered to attend to detail three times (Exod 25:9, 40; 26:30). Why was the construction of this sacred space so important to God? Because this space would be the primary location where he would meet with his people as they worshiped him, "And let them make me a sanctuary, that I may dwell in their midst" (Exod 25:8). As we have previously seen, people in the presence of God are changed—physically and spiritually. Thus, we see that sacred space is an important aspect in our spiritual formation as we worship God.

CONSIDER THIS

Does the church you regularly attend consider sacred space to be important? Based on the design of the worship space, which element of worship would you say is most valued at your church?

Have you ever considered the importance of sacred space to your worship? Is there a "thin place" where God seems most present to you? A church sanctuary . . . the beach . . . the mountains . . . a backyard garden? How can you make that place meaningful in your worship?

FOR FURTHER CONSIDERATION

Ahmanson, Roberta. "The Ramifications of Sacred Space." Lecture presented March 2, 2012 at Art Symposium, Biola University. http://ccca.biola.edu/resources/2016/sep/7/sacred-space/.

Lev, Elizabeth. "The Development of Sacred Space in Rome, The Cradle of Christian Architecture." Lecture presented March 2, 2012 at Art Symposium, Biola University. http://ccca.biola.edu/resources/2012/mar/2/development-sacred-space-rome/.

White, James F., and Susan J. White. Church Architecture: Building and Renovating for Christian Worship. Claremont: OSL, 1998.

Wolterstorff, Nicholas. "Sacred Places, Sacred Space." Lecture presented March 1, 2012 at Art Symposium, Biola University. http://ccca.biola.edu/resources/2014/mar/20/sacred-places-sacred-space-panel-discussion/.

12

Sacred Time and Worship Formation

Look carefully then how you walk, not as unwise but as wise, making the best use of the time, because the days are evil. Therefore do not be foolish, but understand what the will of the Lord is.

—EPHESIANS 5:15-17

DURING MY CHILDHOOD AND adolescence I attended a small conservative evangelical church. It was there that I offered my life to Christ and was baptized. My family committed unreservedly to church. If the doors were open, we were there. For us, that meant all day Sunday (morning service, afternoon choir rehearsal, and evening service) and every Wednesday night for Bible study. My dad was a deacon and served as the church's sound technician. My mom was a Sunday School teacher and sang in the choir. Needless to say, church was a very big part of the routine of our lives.

Spending most of my life in that church, I had no real sense of sacred time in worship. It simply was not practiced as a regular part of the worshiping life of that congregation. Sure, we had Christmas celebrations and Easter Sunday was a pretty big deal, but next to those the biggest celebrations we engaged in were Mother's Day and Father's Day. I had never really even heard the term "sacred time" until college, where I learned of the Christian Year—a calendar of seasons for the church that follows the life of Christ and the subsequent birth and growth of the church. The observance of the seasons of the Christian Year has a long history in the life of the

Christian faith and unites the global church in an opportunity to tell the story of God's redemptive work in the world.

My first reaction to learning of the Christian Year was to refuse to follow an archaic calendar that I believed would inevitably turn my worship into empty rote and ritual. I did not understand how the Christian Year could be used as a component of worship to draw us into a deeper connection with Christ by honoring his life, death, resurrection, and coming return. Thankfully, over time, my understanding and appreciation for the Christian Year has changed. This change of perspective has been a journey for which I am exceedingly grateful.

❖ ❖ ❖

The keeping of sacred time allows Christians the opportunity to develop a pattern in their life that will maintain perpetual spiritual living. Our lives follow a pattern; a rhythm; a cycle. The sun rises and sets, the ocean tides rise and fall, we wake and sleep, we rise up and we lie down, we are born and we die. The question becomes, what, or better yet who, do you want at the center of that cycle? Observing sacred time by following the Christian Year calendar challenges the believer to experience the spiritually transforming power of God by having Christ at the center of our worship.

I believe the main reason for the development of worship issues within the church stems from a culture of narcissism that has found its way into our churches and our worship. In such cases, worship is not primarily about God and what he has done. There is a deepening disregard of the incredible saving act of the One true and holy God and a denial of the fullness of the story of God. Worship therefore becomes all about us—what we like, what we want, and what we feel we deserve. We have bypassed the Almighty, sovereign God, and have positioned our own unworthy selves as the focus of worship. Our worship services have come to reflect this narcissistic attitude when we do not remember the fullness of God's story, either by our choices or training, and are planned according to either the Hallmark or academic calendars.

When worship services are patterned after the Hallmark calendar, they are structured around holidays such as Mother's Day, Father's Day, Independence Day, Valentine's Day, Scout Sunday, etc. Within this calendar observance, greeting-card special occasions have become the foundation of our worship services. However, the worship service of a church should be about remembering God's work done in our lives and anticipating the work he is yet to do. This remembrance and anticipation should be paramount in any gathering. We may well honor moms on Mother's Day and dads on Father's Day, but the primary focus of the worship service must be on worshiping the One who gave us our moms and dads.

The beginning of the school year at times guides our church calendar, resulting in worship services patterned around the academic calendar. We begin our serious studies in the fall when school is in session. Ministries take their annual hiatus during the summer, and church seems to enter maintenance mode until September when school starts up again and ministries resume meeting. This pattern oftentimes creates a lull in the expression of worship throughout the congregation during the summer months as they wait for everything to fall back into a familiar rhythm—as if God deserves any less of our enthusiastic, wholehearted worship in July.

As a result of utilizing either the Hallmark or the academic calendar, churches run the risk of growing weary of a faith that is shaped by the culture and expectations of the world around them. There is danger in following the pattern of the world in terms of our worship. Worship is not intended to remember holidays nor even significant Christian events such as the Reformation. Worship is to celebrate God and to rehearse his marvelous story.

Because God's nature is beyond what we could fathom or comprehend, the Hallmark and academic calendars fall short in leading congregations to worship more fully. Therefore the question arises, how do we worship God to the fullest expression of our being and journey deeper into knowing Christ? I believe one way to worship God most fully is found in the observance of the Christian Year.

When I was a doctoral student, I studied the Christian Year and the impact it has on the church. Consequently, I became a firm believer that our lives can be spiritually formed through observing sacred time living in the reflection of Christ's life, death, and resurrection. The Christian Year tells the fullness of God's story throughout its seasons reflecting upon the life of Christ, and the birth and subsequent growth of the church. This keeping of sacred time is important for the church as many sociologists and academic historians have suggested that the modern West has lost a sense of shared meaning—or sense of story. For many living in the twenty-first century, life feels as though it is a random, unspecified sequence of events without meaningful shape, reliant upon social media snippets and shallow interactions. But the church, which is older and far more encompassing than the modern West, offers a different perspective. Christianity teaches that the universe has an overall story, running from creation until the end of time, expressed in the fullness of Jesus. The Christian Year calendar, which is structured primarily around the life of Christ and secondarily around the lives of his followers, the church, serves to connect our daily lives to this story.

The Christian Year, also called the church year or liturgical year, is the Christian way of marking time. This specific way of marking time includes two main cycles—the Cycle of Light and the Cycle of Life. The Cycle of Light begins with the waiting period of Advent leading into the incarnational wonder of Christmas. These seasons elucidate for us the self-emptying of God (Phil 2:7) as the Son became flesh. The Cycle of Life begins with the penitential nature of Lent and ushers the worshiper into the resurrection reality of Easter. At this point, I believe a brief overview of the Christian Year will benefit our discussion.

THE CYCLE OF LIGHT

Advent

Advent, which is Latin for "coming," begins four Sundays before Christmas Day (December 25) and is the beginning of the Christian Year. In the Old Testament, the people of God waited for the coming of Messiah—his first coming. The primary focus of Advent today, however, has been on what is popularly called "the second coming" as we await the coming of Christ as King. In light of this, the season of Advent must be looked at in reverse—from the end to the beginning. The second coming of Christ explains his first coming as a babe in Bethlehem.

Christmas

Christmas is more than just a one-day celebration on December 25. It is a season which lasts for twelve days from December 25 to January 5. This is where the song "The Twelve Days of Christmas" comes from. The origin for the twelve-day season of Christmas lies in the early church. As early as mid-second century, Christians in the East celebrated the birth of Jesus on January 6. In the West, Christians began to celebrate Christmas on December 25, probably originating in Rome around 336 AD. Eventually, for worshipers in the West, these two dates became bookends for the Christmas season, with the celebration of the birth of Jesus on December 25 representing the beginning of the festival, and the celebration of the manifestation of Christ to the world by the visit of the magi on January 6 (Epiphany) representing the end of the Christmas festival.

Epiphany

Epiphany is a one-day event (called a "feast" in the Christian calendar) occurring on January 6. The general theme of Epiphany and the season that follows is the manifestation of Jesus as God. Epiphany means "manifestation" or "appearance" and primarily remembers two main events: the arrival of the magi as they brought gifts to Jesus of gold (to symbolize his royal standing), frankincense (to symbolize his deity), and myrrh (to symbolize his mortality), as well as the baptism of Jesus (and sometimes his first miracle at Cana of turning water into wine).

Ordinary Time—Season After Epiphany

Ordinary Time does not mean "boring time when nothing interesting happens." The term derives from the word "ordinal," as in "numbered," with the Sundays that fall within Ordinary Time often designated such as The First Sunday After Epiphany, The Second Sunday After Epiphany, and so on. Ordinary Time refers to any period of time that falls outside the major seasons of the Christian Year, commonly referred to as Extraordinary Time. Wherein the times of Christmas and Easter focus our attention on specific aspects of Christ's extraordinary life and what it means to us, during Ordinary Time we think about what Christ means to the entirety of our lives. During the Season After Epiphany, the church considers the ways Jesus was made manifest, or publicly known, to the world. These manifestations include the magi declaring to Herod that they were in search of the newborn King (Matt 2:1–12), Simeon revealing Jesus's identity as he gazed upon the Messiah in the temple (Luke 2:22–24; not to mention the declarations made by Anna the prophetess, Luke 2:36–38), God the Father speaking from heaven while the Spirit descended upon Jesus at his baptism (Luke 3:15–17, 21–22), the miracle of turning water into wine resulting in the disciples' belief (John 2:1–11), and the transfiguration of Jesus with the voice of God the Father once again speaking from heaven to earth (Mark 9:2–9; Matt 17:1–3; Luke 9:28–36). Epiphany (January 6) and the Season After Epiphany runs from the close of the Christmas season to the beginning of Lent.

THE CYCLE OF LIFE

Lent

Lent is a forty-day period (based on the forty days of temptation that Jesus faced in the wilderness: see Matthew 4:1–11) of fasting, prayer, self-examination, and repentance, in anticipation of the day Christ sacrificed himself on the cross for the sins of all mankind. The term Lent means "springtime." Just as the season of spring within the solar calendar encourages what's often called spring cleaning,[1] the season of Lent within the church calendar is a time to engage in the "spring cleaning" of our souls. It is a time to search within ourselves, and even more, to allow God to search within us and take away anything that does not give him glory, inviting Christ to dwell in its place (Ps 139:23–24). Lent is a season for personal and corporate spiritual renewal, including times of intense study of God's word, meditation, prayer, and self-examination. The Lenten season lasts from Ash Wednesday to Easter Sunday.

Holy Week

This is the last full week of Lent, but is emphasized separately because of the awesome and terrible events that unfolded between the days of Palm Sunday (when Jesus entered Jerusalem to the praise of the people) and Holy Saturday (when Jesus was in the tomb after his crucifixion on Friday). Holy Week includes what is known as The Great Triduum, or The Great Three Days. These days include Maundy Thursday (Maundy means "mandate" or "command"; this is the day of Jesus's last supper with his disciples), Good Friday (the use of the word good here means "holy" as in the Friday within Holy Week; this is the day Jesus was crucified), and Holy Saturday or the Paschal Vigil (an observance of prayer and waiting in preparation for the celebration of the resurrection of Jesus; this is the day Jesus lay in the tomb).

---

1. Spring cleaning is a housekeeping ritual that takes place in the spring, emerging from times when winter left homes coated with a layer of soot and grime due to being heated with wood and coal devices. Proper cleaning required opening windows to let the soot out, which, of course, could only be done during warmer weather, which started in spring.

Easter

Easter is the greatest celebration of the Christian Year because it is the most important event in all of history—the glorious resurrection of Jesus Christ. During these days, which last fifty days overall, the church that observes the Christian Year calendar celebrates Christ's resurrection, remembers the post-resurrection appearances of Christ, celebrates Christ's ascension into heaven and the coming of the Spirit at Pentecost, and begins to explore the implications of the resurrection for the future of God's kingdom. Christ the Lord is risen, alleluia!

Pentecost

Pentecost is the last day of the Easter season, the fiftieth day after Easter, which is the meaning of Pentecost, "fiftieth." This Sunday celebrates the occasion of the Holy Spirit descending upon Christ's disciples as referenced in Acts 2.

Ordinary Time—Season After Pentecost

The Season After Pentecost lasts until the first Sunday of Advent. Themes to consider during this period of Ordinary Time are the birth and subsequent growth of the church and how we are to allow God's story to impact and transform our lives.

Additionally, there are many special days found within the Christian Year calendar called "holy days." Some of these include Ash Wednesday (the first day of the season of Lent), the Baptism of the Lord (usually celebrated on The First Sunday After Epiphany), Trinity Sunday (The First Sunday After Pentecost when we celebrate the triune God—Father, Son, and Holy Spirit), and Christ the King Sunday (the Sunday before the season of Advent when we honor Christ as King of kings and Lord of lords, focusing on anticipating Christ's kingly return when he will reign over all).

The seasons of the Christian Year embolden formation in the life of the worshiper—Advent and Lent are times of preparation and expectation; Christmas and Easter are times of celebration and rejoicing; the feast of

Epiphany and the Season After Pentecost are times of revelation, helping us deepen our faith.

During these times, we come together in congregational worship to remember Christ's saving acts, allowing this remembrance to affect the way we live and worship. Thus, the Christian Year is an instrument by which we are shaped. Throughout our lives we have developed habits by the way we mark and use our time. A spiritual life formed around the Christian Year is designed to form our habits around following Jesus. Yet, it is not the Christian Year that is the basis of our journey of being formed spiritually, but Christ himself in us who forms us, while being mindful of the content and meaning of the Christian Year. The observance of the Christian Year offers the worshiper an opportunity to live in the pattern of Christ's life, death, and resurrection, ushering us toward Christ himself.

At the same time, care has to be taken in order that the Christian Year does not become simply ritualistic in itself. The Christian Year is a great resource to help the worshiper be formed into the likeness of Christ, but like all elements of worship, it should be viewed as a vehicle for us to properly respond to the revelations of God, not a means unto itself. We are reminded of Amos and God's response to the people's worship. The people of Israel were diligent in their worship practices. They were wholehearted in their duties and emotionally satisfied with their offerings to God. However, religious practices do not guarantee engagement with God. In Amos 5, we read about God's rebuke of the people: "I hate, I despise your feasts, and I take no delight in your solemn assemblies" (Amos 5:21). Religion and ritual themselves cannot take the place of a relationship with God, essential for spiritual formation. Nevertheless, the Christian Year offers a foundation for our worship as we approach the throne of mercy in awe and reverence.

Theologian Robert Webber suggests that because we live in a time of cultural and spiritual transition, many Christians are searching for a deeper worship experience than the non-connected church provides: "Many younger evangelicals and older ones as well are searching the past to find ways of spiritual formation that have deeply affected the spiritual lives of many generations."[2] The value of connecting us with our past while moving toward the future is both spiritually formative and unifying. Sacred time is one such element that, when observed, encourages us toward a life that deeply connects with Christ.

---

2. Webber, *Ancient-Future Time*, 15.

By observing the Christian Year in public worship we highlight and promote spiritual formation. Indeed, the motivation of the Christian Year is to relive the major events in Jesus's life in real time as biblical scholar Andrew Hill states, "The purpose of the church year is to sanctify time within the yearly experience of church life. The celebration of Christ's life, teaching, death, resurrection, ascension, and sending of the Holy Spirit was designed to bring spiritual renewal to the church."[3] It is a time for us to relive for ourselves the saving events of Christ and the presence of the Holy Spirit in our lives. James F. White states, "When we recall the past events of salvation, they come alive in their present power to save. Our acts of remembrance have the potential of bringing the original events back to us with all their meaning. And so, we continue to 'proclaim the Lord's death until he comes' (1 Cor 11:26)."[4] A present encounter with God through the remembrance of past events is the purpose behind the Christian Year. In recalling the saving events of Christ, we do not take a trip in a time machine into the past, nor drag the past into the present by repeating the ancient event through a mythic drama. These events are history, not myth. Nevertheless, though the events of the Christian Year may be in the past, their reality is ever-present, reaching to each new generation; after all, the promise was made "to you and to your descendants, forever" (Gen 13:15).

So in remembering the past, we neither return to it nor do we recreate it in the present. Just as God is ever present, his past saving events are to be remembered as true for all time. The past, present, and future are always relevant in God's time. "Christmas is not just about the coming of Christ to Bethlehem, but about the coming of Christ to me, and about my going out to others. And Easter is not about the empty tomb in Jerusalem some 2000 years ago, but about the reawakening here and now of my baptismal death and resurrection in Christ."[5]

There is a danger in not remembering all God has done for us as well as for those throughout history. Nehemiah shares of the prayer of confession offered by the Israelites, "But our ancestors acted arrogantly; they became stiff-necked and did not listen to your commands. They refused to listen and did not remember your wonders you performed among them" (Neh 9:16–17a, Holman Christian Study Bible). I remember

3. Hill, *Enter His Courts With Praise!*, 93.

4. White, *Introduction to Christian Worship*, 68.

5. Taft, *Beyond East and West*, 18.

watching a television show about the shapes of the States of the United States of America. The host and a historian were talking about a specific state when the historian said that the state has "historical amnesia." They forgot the history of the state and it has affected the way they currently live. I believe the church has the same problem. The church too has historical amnesia. We must understand that worship past is connected to worship present. Our worship is most powerful when we remember God's mighty acts.

An observance of the Christian Year has the potential to direct our worship. Theologian Marva Dawn claims, "Our worship is made much richer when we let the nature of each particular season guide our choices of songs, accompaniments, texts, sermon themes, prayers, drama, art."[6] In my undergraduate classes, I often ask my students if they know the significance of the Sunday before Easter? Some of them do while others do not. Once we establish that this particular Sunday in the Christian Year is what's known as Palm or Passion Sunday,[7] the day Jesus entered Jerusalem while the crowd shouted "Hosanna! Blessed is he who comes in the name of the Lord!" (Mark 11:9), I then ask them to tell me what songs should be sung in our worship services on that day. Since this day was a joyful celebration, as well as the beginning steps toward the fulfillment of Jesus's mission of bringing a glorious salvation to his followers by way of his death on the cross, worshipers can sing songs that triumphantly celebrate this salvation and freedom found in Christ. Therefore, songs that mention hosanna, celebration, triumph, victory, and salvation would be appropriate for this specific day in the Christian Year.

Similarly, do we consider the ascension of Jesus, forty days after his resurrection, to be significant? After all, Jesus's ascension affirms his claims that he will "go to prepare a place for [us]" (John 14:2) and the Scriptures clarify that he now intercedes on our behalf from the throne of heaven in his exalted life above (Rom 8:34; John 17:22; Heb 7:25). If we believe the ascension of Jesus to be an important theological feature of God's story, how do we acknowledge it in our worship services? What songs, prayers, Scripture readings, etc., will we use to provide our congregation the opportunity

6. Dawn, *How Shall We Worship?*, 33.

7. This particular Sunday conveys both the triumphal entry of Jesus into Jerusalem, with the crowd waving palm fronds and laying down their cloaks before him on the road (hence the title "Palm Sunday"), and Jesus looking over the city and weeping knowing he has begun his focused journey to the cross to fulfill the crowd's cries of "Hosanna," meaning "save" (hence the title "Passion Sunday").

to respond in worship in ways that are mindful of the ascension? Observing the Christian Year reminds us of the parts of the gospel story we often forget or neglect and offers structure to our worship providing occasions to recognize the fullness of the story of God. There is depth to the Christian Year leading those that observe it to open themselves to allowing their lives to be formed spiritually by its practice.

A resurgence of sacred time in our worship has the ability to invite us into a life ready to embrace spiritual formation. The early Christians believed all time found its meaning in the death and resurrection of Jesus Christ. They allowed their lives to be shaped by the saving events of Christ. They epitomized Paul's words: "For me to live is Christ" (Phil 1:21), and they demonstrated how lives can be ordered through the discipline of keeping sacred time. As Robert Webber articulately states,

> Christian Year spirituality is nothing less than the calling to enter by faith into the incarnation, the life and ministry, the death and resurrection of Jesus. God's saving action is not only presented to us through the practice of the Christian Year, it also takes up residence within us and transforms us by the saving and healing presence of Christ in our lives.[8]

Observing sacred time is a practical way of being more truly formed into the likeness of Christ. It provides spiritual refreshment by giving order to our lives. Believers will naturally take on a different perspective as their lives are ordered around the life of Christ, bringing unity with Christ and with one another.

Since worship is a rehearsing of God's story, then keeping sacred time would enable the church to recall the story on a consistent basis throughout the year. The observance of the seasons of the Christian Year has a long history in the life of the Christian faith and continues to usher us toward God's story dramatically shaping who we are and the way we worship today. Planned and purposeful observances of the seasons of the church can become an important vehicle for spiritual formation and vitality within the congregation.

8. Webber, *Ancient-Future Time*, 27.

CONSIDER THIS

If you attend a church that observes the Christian Year as part of the worshiping life of your congregation, consider ways in which you can help bring a fresh approach to the seasons of the year. Ask the question, "How can we creatively help people experience the richness of our faith through the signs and symbols that have been passed down through the centuries by way of the Christian Year?"

For those who do not attend a church that observes the comprehensive Christian Year, think of a season that your church does not currently observe (Advent, Lent, the full Easter season, etc.). Now think of ways to encourage your congregation to consider the spiritual emphasis behind that specific season. In what ways can you incorporate elements of worship that may assist in making the season a spiritually formative aspect of your congregation's worship? Is there any teaching that needs to occur for your congregation to understand the season? What elements from church tradition (old and recent) can you utilize that enhances the theme of the season?

FOR FURTHER CONSIDERATION

Gross, Bobby. *Living the Christian Year: Time to Inhabit the Story of God*. Downers Grove: InterVarsity, 2009.

Johnson, Maxwell E., ed. *Between Memory and Hope: Readings on the Liturgical Year*. Collegeville: The Liturgical Press, 2000.

Stookey, Laurence H. *Calendar: Christ's Time for the Church*. Nashville: Abingdon, 1996.

Talley, Thomas J. *The Origins of the Liturgical Year*. Collegeville: Liturgical Press, 1986.

Webber, Robert E. *Ancient-Future Time: Forming Spirituality Through the Christian Year*. Grand Rapids: Baker, 2004.

Conclusion

...assuming that you have heard about [Christ] and were taught in him, as the truth is in Jesus, to put off your old self, which belongs to your former manner of life and is corrupt through deceitful desires, and to be renewed in the spirit of your minds, and to put on the new self, created after the likeness of God in true righteousness and holiness.

—Ephesians 4:21–24

Beloved, we are God's children now, and what we will be has not yet appeared; but we know that when he appears we shall be like him, because we shall see him as he is.

—1 John 3:2

Whether we realize it or not, we are spiritually formed as we respond to the revelations made clear by God. The singing of songs, praying of prayers, reading of his holy Scripture, hearing of a sermon, observing of communion, practicing stillness, participating in baptism, and more, forms our hearts, renews our minds, and transforms our lives. The church has always believed that God is not only present everywhere but that he is also made present to his church in worship. When the church of God gathers together and responds to God through acts of worship, God is there and his Spirit is at work forming worshipers.

Worship formation is the process by which our inner beings are being opened and connected to God in deep and meaningful ways. If we consider the life of the worshiper being a sort of timeline with "New Believer" (the day of acceptance of Jesus Christ as Lord and Savior) on one end and "New Body" (the day of crossing the threshold between earth and heaven either through death or Christ's return) on the opposite end, we see that every worshiper is at a different place in the process—on the timeline. As we worship together, each person is encouraged by the Holy Spirit to move one step closer toward being like Jesus—a journey that continues until the day we receive the "New Body."[1]

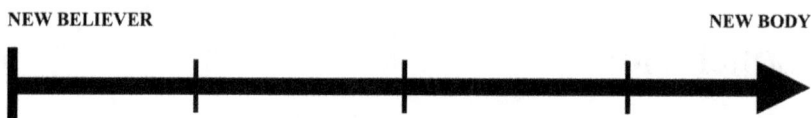

NEW BELIEVER   **NEW BODY**

Is your worship moving you in the right direction?

We are not bystanders in this process of spiritual formation. We are active participants with God, who is inviting us into deeper relationship with him through worship. Worship offered in spirit and truth, that forms us well, will move us toward Christ-likeness, while poor responses to God keep us stagnate, or worst yet, move us further away from a right relationship with Christ. While churches everywhere are looking for the latest and greatest discipleship program in an effort to revitalize their congregations, I believe the best option is found in spiritually formative worship.

Worship formation is the building up of our spiritual lives much like training in a gym is the building up of our physical bodies. The apostle Paul encourages Timothy to help the church "train yourself to be godly. For physical training is of some value, but godliness has value for all things, holding promise for both the present life and the life to come" (1 Tim 4:7–8). Just as discipling our bodies through physical exercise strengthens our muscles and increases our physical health, practicing the spiritual disciplines of worship strengthens our spiritual muscles and increases spiritual health and maturity. It is training in eternal living by the power of the

1. It is clear that every follower of Christ will receive a new body (Phil 3:20–21). There is not a question as to whether or not that transformation will ultimately occur. Here rather, in light of worship formation, we are discussing the theological concept of sanctification. According to the Westminster Shorter Catechism (Q. 35), sanctification is "the work of God's free grace, whereby we are renewed in the whole man after the image of God, and are enabled more and more to die unto sin, and live unto righteousness." As worshipers, our desire should be that when it is time to receive the new body, we are as close to being like Christ as possible. Anything less is not an offering of wholehearted worship to the Lord.

Holy Spirit that leads to becoming the disciples that Jesus desires and the worshipers the Father is seeking.

In summary, God desires for us to be open to his Spirit forming us at any time, in any place, and in every way as each element of worship within a worship service leads the worshiper to be:

> . . . transformed by the renewal of your mind, that by testing you may discern what is the will of God. (Rom 12:2)

As we worship God, we are spiritually formed becoming more like Christ, and thereby, we are engaged in *worship formation*.

Bibliography

Archbishop John. "Sacred Music: Its Nature and Function." *Word Magazine*, February 1989.

Bainton, Roland H. *Here I Stand: A Life of Martin Luther.* Peabody: Hendrickson, 1950.

Barna, George. *Revolution: Finding Vibrant Faith Beyond the Walls of the Sanctuary.* Wheaton: Tyndale, 2005.

———. *Today's Pastors: A Revealing Look At What Pastors Are Saying About Themselves, Their Peers, and the Pressures They Face.* Ventura: Regal, 1993.

Bateman, Herbert W., IV. *Authentic Worship: Hearing Scripture's Voice, Applying Its Truths.* Grand Rapids: Kregel, 2002.

Best, Harold M. *Unceasing Worship: Biblical Perspectives on Worship and the Arts.* Downers Grove: InterVarsity, 2003.

Block, Daniel I. *For the Glory of God: Recovering A Biblical Theology of Worship.* Grand Rapids: Baker Academic, 2014.

Brooks, Steven D. *Worship Quest: An Exploration of Worship Leadership.* Eugene: Wipf & Stock, 2015.

Brown, Rosalind. *How Hymns Shape Our Lives.* Cambridge: Grove, 2001.

Cairns, Frank. *The Prophet of the Heart.* London: Hodder and Stoughton, 1934.

Chan, Simon. *Liturgical Theology: The Church as Worshiping Community.* Downers Grove: InterVarsity, 2006.

Cherry, Constance. "My House Shall Be Called a House of . . . Announcements." http://alumni.iws.edu/pdf/Cherry%20article%20My%20House.pdf.

———. *The Worship Architect: A Blueprint for Designing Culturally Relevant and Biblically Faithful Services.* Grand Rapids: Baker Academic, 2010.

Cherry, Constance, et al. *Selecting Worship Songs: A Guide for Leaders.* Marion, IN: Triangle, 2011.

Church of England. *Common Worship: Services and Prayers for the Church of England.* London: Church House, 2000.

Cyril, Saint. *Lectures on the Christian Sacraments.* Crestwood: St. Vladimir's Seminary Press, 1951.

Dawn, Marva J. *How Shall We Worship? Biblical Guidelines for the Worship Wars.* Wheaton: Tyndale, 2003.

Fee, Gordon D. *Philippians.* The IVP New Testament Commentary Series. Downers Grove: InterVarsity, 1999.

Furr, Gary, and Milburn Price. *The Dialogue of Worship: Creating Space for Revelation and Response.* Macon: Smyth and Helwys, 1998.

Deans, Graham D. S. "Short Guide No 27: Hymns and Ministry to Those with Dementia." https://hymnsocietygbi.org.uk/2017/03/short-guide-no-27-hymns-and-ministry-to-those-with-dementia/.

Guinness, Os. *No God but God: Breaking with the Idols of Our Age*. Chicago: Moody, 1992.

Hill, Andrew E. *Enter His Courts With Praise! Old Testament Worship for the New Testament Church*. Grand Rapids: Baker, 1993.

Hippolytus, Saint. *The Treatise on the Apostolic Tradition of Saint Hippolytus of Rome*. Edited by Gregory Dix. 2nd ed. London, SPCK, 1968.

Hustad, Donald P. *Jubilate! Church Music in the Evangelical Tradition*. Carol Stream: Hope, 1981.

Lawson, Tom. "The Magic Story." *Adorate (Worship)*, September 2012. http://adorate.blogspot.com/2012/09/the-magic-story.html.

Lucas, Cheri. "Boost Memory and Learning with Music." https://www.pbs.org/parents/thrive/boost-memory-and-learning-with-music.

Mains, Karen B. *Sing Joyfully!* Carol Stream: Tabernacle, 1989.

Martyr, Justin. *The First and Second Apologies*. Edited by Walter J. Burghardt et al. Translated by Leslie William Barnard. Ancient Christian Writers. New York: Paulist, 1997.

Merton, Thomas. *The Way of Chuang Tzu*. The Abbey of Gethsemani: New Directions, 1965.

Miller, Kevin A, ed. "The Reformer's Early Years." *Christian History (Quarterly)* 11.2 (1992) 2–51.

Nouwen, Henri J. M. *In the Name of Jesus: Reflections on Christian Leadership*. New York: Crossroad, 1989.

———. *The Way of the Heart: Connecting with God Through Prayer, Wisdom, and Silence*. New York: Seabury, 1981.

———. *With Burning Hearts: A Meditation on the Eucharistic Life*. Maryknoll: Orbis, 1994.

Old, Hughes Oliphant. *Leading in Prayer: A Workbook for Worship*. Grand Rapids: Eerdmans, 1995.

Oldenburg, Ray. *The Great Good Place: Cafés, Coffee Shops, Bookstores, Bars, Hair Salons, and Other Hangouts at the Heart of the Community*. New York: Marlowe & Company, 1989.

Orthodox Presbyterian Church. *Trinity Hymnal*. Philadelphia: Great Commission, 1961.

Packer, J. I. *Beyond the Battle for the Bible*. Wheaton: Crossway, 1980.

Parbery-Clark, A., et al. "Musical Experience and Hearing Loss: Perceptual, Cognitive and Neural Benefits in Association for Research in Otolaryngology Symposium." PLoS One 6.5 (2011) e18082.

Postema, Don. *Space for God: Study and Practice of Spirituality and Prayer*. Grand Rapids: Faith Alive, 1997.

Pottie, Charles S. *A More Profound Alleluia! Gelineau and Routley on Music in Christian Worship*. Washington, DC: Pastoral Press, 1984.

Putnam, Robert D. *Bowling Alone: The Collapse and Revival of American Community*. New York: Simon & Schuster, 2000.

Ralston, Timothy J. "Scripture in Worship: An Indispensable Symbol of Covenant." In *Authentic Worship: Hearing Scripture's Voice, Applying Its Truth*, edited by Herbert W. Bateman IV, 195–224. Grand Rapids: Kregal, 2002.

Roberts, Mark D. "Thin Places: Theological Reflections and Hesitations." *Mark D. Roberts: Reflections on Christ, Church, and Culture*, 2012. http://www.patheos.com/blogs/markdroberts/series/thin-places/.

Ruth, Lester. "Don't Lose the Trinity! A Plea to Songwriters." http://alumni.iws.edu/resources/Trinity%20in%20Song-Ruth.htm.

Segler, Franklin M., and Randall Bradley. *Christian Worship: Its Theology and Practice.* Nashville: B&H, 2006.

Smith, James K. A. *Desiring the Kingdom: Worship, Worldview, and Cultural Formation.* Grand Rapids: Baker Academic, 2009.

———. *You Are What You Love: The Spiritual Power of Habit.* Grand Rapids: Brazos, 2016.

Soukup, Charles. "Computer-Mediated Communication as a Virtual Third Place: Building Oldenburg's Great Good Places on the World Wide Web." *Journal of Computer-Mediated Communication* 8.3 (June 1, 2006) 421–40.

Sproul, R. C. *The Holiness of God.* Carol Stream: Tyndale House, 1985.

Spurgeon, Charles. "Magnificat." https://www.spurgeon.org/resource-library/sermons/magnificat#flipbook/.

Taft, Robert F. *Beyond East and West: Problems in Liturgical Understanding.* Rome: Pontifical Oriental Institute, 2001.

Torrance, Thomas. *Conflict and Agreement in the Church.* Eugene: Wipf and Stock, 1996.

Tozer, A. W. *Whatever Happened To Worship?* Camp Hill: Christian Publications, 1985.

Vander Zee, Leonard J. *Christ, Baptism and the Lord's Supper: Recovering the Sacraments for Evangelical Worship.* Downers Grove: InterVarsity, 2004.

Ward, Benedicta, trans. *The Sayings of the Desert Fathers.* London & Oxford: Mowbrays, 1975.

Webber, Robert E. *Ancient-Future Time: Forming Spirituality Through the Christian Year.* Grand Rapids: Baker, 2004.

———. *Ancient-Future Worship: Proclaiming and Enacting God's Narrative.* Grand Rapids: Baker, 2008.

———. *Worship Is a Verb: Eight Principles for Transforming Worship.* Peabody: Hendrickson, 1985.

White, James F. *Introduction to Christian Worship.* 3rd ed. Nashville: Abingdon, 2000.

Wiersbe, Warren W. *Real Worship: Playground, Battle Ground, or Holy Ground?* Grand Rapids: Baker, 2000.

Willard, Dallas, and Jan Johnson. *Renovation of the Heart in Daily Practice: Experiments in Spiritual Transformation.* Colorado Springs: NavPress, 2006.

Willimon, William. *The Service of God: How Worship and Ethics are Related.* Nashville: Abingdon, 1983.

"Worship Leader Commits 47 Heresies in 30-Second Prayer." *Babylon Bee*, October 18, 2018. https://babylonbee.com/news/worship-leader-commits-47-heresies-in-30-second-prayer.

Wright, N. T. *The Last Word.* New York: HarperCollins, 2005.